NOWHERE TO RUN

The Killing of
Constable Dennis Strongquill

By Mike McIntyre

GREAT PLAINS
PUBLICATIONS

Great Plains Publications
420 – 70 Arthur Street
Winnipeg, MB R3B 1G7
www.greatplains.mb.ca

Great Plains Publications gratefully acknowledges the financial
support provided for its publishing program by the Government of
Canada through the Book Publishing Industry Development
Program (BPIDP); the Canada Council for the Arts; as well as the
Manitoba Department of Culture, Heritage and Tourism; and the
Manitoba Arts Council.

Design & Typography by Gallant Design Ltd.
Printed in Canada by Kromar Printing Ltd.

CANADIAN CATALOGUING IN PUBLICATION DATA

Main entry under title:
McIntyre, Mike
  Nowhere to run : the killing of Constable Dennis Strongquill /
Mike McIntyre.

ISBN 1-894283-44-9

1. Strongquill, Dennis, 1949-2001.   2. Murder–Manitoba–Russell.
3. Trials (Murder)–Manitoba–Brandon.   4. Sand, Robert Marlo–
Trials, litigation, etc.   5. Bell, Laurie Ann–Trials, litigation, etc.
I.   Title
HV6535.C33R87 2003   364.15'23   C2003-911162-8

For Chassity

INTRODUCTION

This book is based entirely on actual events. All the material has been derived from the following sources: witness testimony at the first-degree murder trial of Robert Sand and Laurie Bell, held April through June 2003 in Brandon, Manitoba; official court records, including documents tendered as evidence at trial and transcripts; previously published reports on the case; a jailhouse interview with Robert Sand at Stony Mountain Penitentiary in July 2003; numerous interviews conducted with family, friends and associates of Robert and Danny Sand, and Laurie Bell; extensive interviews with family, friends, neighbours and colleagues of Dennis Strongquill; lengthy discussions, both pre- and post-trial, with Crown prosecutor Bob Morrison and defence lawyer Greg Brodsky; and personal visits to the majority of cities, towns and communities mentioned in this book, including Westlock, Clyde, Athabasca, Edmonton, Barrows, Russell and Waywayseecappo.

I would like to personally thank all the people who opened up their homes, and hearts, to discuss this tragic case in preparation for this project. Special acknowledgment to the families of Dennis Strongquill and of Robert and Danny Sand, for allowing me into their lives under very trying circumstances. Both families have suffered horrible losses, and have my sympathy. Also, to the city of Brandon, which became a second home for me in the spring of 2003 and always made me feel welcome. This was a difficult and emotional case for everyone involved, but the city's first-class hospitality left me returning home to Winnipeg with some fond memories.

A special thank-you to Kim Guttormson, whose talent, generosity and guidance will never be forgotten.

I dedicate this book to my family, whose strength, support and unconditional love have helped guide me through a world which isn't always fair and doesn't always make sense. My beautiful wife, Chassity, for being my rock and foundation; my wonderful son, Parker, a true Angel who shows me every day why life is special; my parents, Ted and Susan, for always believing in me; my brother, Stephen, for dedicating his life to helping others; and Nanny, my biggest fan with a heart as pure as gold.

I would also like to honour the brave men and women who police our streets and highways on a daily basis, putting their own safety at risk in what is truly a thankless job. You have my thanks, as well as my respect and admiration.

ACKNOWLEDGEMENTS

This book was made possible with the help and understanding of the following:

Chassity McIntyre, Parker McIntyre, Ted McIntyre, Susan McIntyre, Stephen McIntyre, Kim Guttormson, Nadia Moharib, Phyllis Scott, Bruce Owen, Charles Adler, David Staples, Bob Morrison, Nicholas Hirst, Steve Pona, Larry Kusch, Jon Thordarson, and Adriano Magnifico.

PROLOGUE

The clock had struck midnight, but 2 a.m. still seemed a long way off for a couple of policemen who had pulled this graveyard shift too many times.

House lights were turned off, the streets and highways of western Manitoba were deserted, save for the odd semi-trailer trying to press on into the night, and the only excitement to be had was trying to predict how much snow would blanket the area.

Royal Canadian Mounted Police constables Dennis Strongquill and Brian Auger drove through the darkness, eyes open for trouble that neither man expected to find four days before Christmas.

Even an earlier walk through the often rambunctious Waywayseecappo Inn gaming lounge hadn't produced anything more than a few curious glances. Not even a dimwitted drunk to liven up the night.

Six hours had passed. Two more to go. It felt like an eternity.

With the largely Aboriginal community of Waywayseecappo safely tucked away for the night, Brian suggested they head to Russell for a coffee. He was always coming up with good ideas, and Dennis wasn't going to argue with how good a hot cup of java would feel right now.

It didn't matter that Russell was 30 kilometres away, and that the only option was the local Subway restaurant, which stayed open late for sandwich-craving nighthawks and working stiffs. It was a perfect way to pass the time.

Besides, the men were expecting company. Jennifer Pashe, a breath of fresh air who recently joined their tiny detachment, had promised to meet them during the night should they find time for a break. And there was plenty of time on this night.

With Christmas just around the corner, there would be lots to talk about. Dennis's new baby daughter, Korrie, would surely be a hot topic. The six-week-old girl didn't know it, but she was about to celebrate her first-ever holiday, along with Dennis and girlfriend Mandy Delorande.

Dennis, despite being a new father at 52 years of age, resembled a kid himself when proudly telling others about Korrie, the new girl in his life.

Brian, sitting behind the wheel of the RCMP Ford Explorer, turned westbound on to Highway 45, a desolate stretch of road in the dead of a winter's night, and headed towards Russell. Destination, Subway.

Brian eased up on the gas, noting the weather was changing from a misty fog to light snowfall. Traction was good, but why risk it? There was no rush.

The coffee would still be hot.

As the windshield wipers fought back the increasingly heavy snowfall, Brian and Dennis finally saw a sign of life on the Prairies.

Up ahead, just beside the Russell golf course, a vehicle appeared. Dennis and Brian paid little attention at first, but were drawn to the vehicle as it was coming off a gravel road.

Facing north, the vehicle appeared to go straight through the stop sign before turning east on to the highway.

Brian and Dennis squinted as the strong glare of the headlights hit their wet windshield.

The high beams were on. Not unusual, given the long stretches one could travel through the darkened countryside without seeing another vehicle.

Brian and Dennis tried to look inside the vehicle, but the lights were stinging their eyes, preventing them from getting a good look.

The officers expected the lights to dim. They didn't.

It took only seconds for the truck to go by them and then re-appear in their rear-view mirror.

How rude, the officers thought. Brian told Dennis he was going to pull the vehicle over. They might have let the stop sign infraction slide. But temporarily blinding them was obnoxious.

The coffee could wait.

Brian quickly turned the Explorer around, and flicked on his flashing exterior emergency lights. The truck drove less than a mile before Brian and Dennis saw the red brake lights, indicating the occupants of the truck were willing to stop.

Highway traffic stops, particularly at night, always gave Brian and Dennis a sense of anxiety, especially on shifts where they had worked alone. It was the fear of the unknown that would often leave them feeling vulnerable.

Both men, with more than 20 years of service each, knew the prompt stopping of the vehicle was a good sign. It's the ones who run, or try to get clever, that you had to worry about.

The truck rolled to a stop on the shoulder of the blustery highway. Brian pulled his vehicle, emergency lights still flashing, about 15 feet behind, taking note of an Alberta licence plate. Maybe some out-of-towners who had come home for the holidays, the officers thought.

As Dennis began to open his passenger side door, a figure emerged from the passenger side of the truck. He marched from his truck and towards the police vehicle, where Dennis and Brian were still seated. He moved with a purpose, taking brisk steps in the snow.

The figure raised his arms, up towards his head. Dennis remained inside, his door still ajar.

Suddenly, there was a loud flash of light, and a shot boomed against the front windshield. Then another. And another.

Dennis quickly slammed his door shut.

"Back up! Reverse. Back up," he shouted at his partner.

Dennis didn't even have a chance to draw his gun before Brian had the car moving, rapidly. Brian drove backwards about 100 feet. At the same time, he activated an emergency button on his police radio, alerting dispatchers in Winnipeg they were under attack.

Brian and Dennis watched in shock as the gunman retreated to his truck, which then whipped around and, unbelievably, headed straight for them.

Brian followed his instincts and spun the Explorer around, speeding towards Russell at 130 km-h, the truck still visible in his rear-view mirror.

It was 12:31 a.m. Less than an hour and a half until their shift was over. But Brian and Dennis were no longer thinking about what time they punched out.

Grabbing his hand-held radio from his belt, Dennis called a dispatcher in Winnipeg who wanted to know where he and his partner were. The dispatcher had seen their emergency button activated and was worried.

"There's a vehicle following us," Dennis said, a sense of panic in his voice.

The operator asked for their location. Dennis didn't respond immediately, as the sounds of gunshots striking the police car were taking up the bulk of his attention.

"We're hit!" Dennis told the dispatcher.

Brian raced towards town, the truck still on their tail. Dennis was working the radio as shots continued to hit the car. The shooters were getting closer, with the rear windshield exploding and pellets beating against the Plexiglas shield separating the rear and front seats of the car.

The long pauses between radio transmissions had Dennis worried. Brian approached the town of Russell, hitting the intersections of Highway 45 and Highway 16, then turning sharply down Main Street. The truck was now closer than ever, tailgating the shot-up police car with its broken glass and missing windows.

It was 12:34 a.m. Dennis, increasingly frantic, tried to rouse nearby officers, but in rural detachments, nearby could mean 50 kilometres or farther.

"Shot at, we're being shot at, guys. We're being shot at. You hear that…shootin' us. They're still shootin' us," he yelled into the radio.

Brian couldn't return fire, focused instead on keeping his vehicle on the increasingly slippery highway. Dennis had his nine-millimetre S & W pistol out, but it was of no use. The magazine clip had somehow been jolted, causing his ammunition to fall to the ground. It was too dark, and too hectic, for him to retrieve it. They had also neglected to place the police-issue 12 gauge back in the dash mount when they had left the detachment.

Brian raced for the detachment, counting on collecting superior weapons to their handguns and hoping some other officers might be inside. The chase was nearly over, and Brian and Dennis agreed to bail out of their car and run to the detachment when they couldn't drive any closer.

Brian made an abrupt turn off Main Street into a snow-filled ditch, but the truck remained directly behind him. He headed directly towards the main building, but was forced to slow down, then stop, as a line of trees he hadn't counted on got in his way.

Brian began to open his door, but was thrown into the snow when the gunmen's truck broadsided Dennis's side of the car. Dennis, still fumbling for his pistol, was wedged in his seat by the crumpled door.

Gunfire erupted again. Brian believed he was going to die as he lay in the snow, his partner trapped inside the car.

There was a series of bright muzzle flashes from Dennis's side of the car, but Brian could hear no sounds.

Brian struggled to his feet on the driver's side and saw three people inside the Alberta truck, which was still pressed against the police car. He quickly scanned the area for Dennis but couldn't see him.

Pistol firmly in hand, Brian raced towards the truck and took aim at the driver.

He fired into the vehicle, over and over and over again. Twelve shots in all. He was trying to hit anyone he could.

Brian was fighting this battle alone, unaware of the fate of his long-time partner. Despite receiving a hail of gunfire, the truck started to move again, as Brian continued pumping bullets inside. It took mere seconds for the truck to turn around and disappear behind the tree line into the night.

Where was Dennis? Brian ran back to the cruiser and saw the constable slumped over the console between the seats.

At first, Brian couldn't see any obvious signs of injury. Then he noticed a gaping bloody hole in the back of Dennis's heavy winter coat.

CHAPTER ONE

"**S**orry I was late. I ran into an old friend."

Maybe it was the way Robert Sand said it, or the way his eyes looked when he spoke. Either way, Elisabeth Colbourne knew something was up. The day was half-over, a day they had planned to spend furniture shopping, picking out Christmas presents for their parents, pigging out on fast food, just catching up, and Robert had just arrived at her downtown Edmonton apartment, hours later than promised, with a mysterious excuse. Elisabeth had been pacing around her modest suite all morning, putting away dishes, checking her e-mail, re-arranging couch pillows, anything to pass the time, not wanting to think the worst. This was Robert, after all. Mr. Unpredictable. But for all his faults, she could always count on him to be on time whenever he came to visit. Not today, though.

Elisabeth wanted to know more, worried that something had happened, that Robert had given into temptation and done something stupid. He looked fine, albeit somewhat distracted. *At least he's not back in jail*, she thought. After giving her a hug, like always, Robert had quickly changed the subject, clearly not wanting to talk about what had kept him so long. Elisabeth knew all too well how precious their time together was, so there was no sense wasting more of it by having an argument. They certainly had done enough of that in the past.

As a couple, Robert and Elisabeth were as mismatched as they come. Elisabeth, the prim and proper Catholic school girl; Robert, the wild-eyed, long-haired rebel without a cause. Their differences helped bring them together, but also had driven them apart. Long-time neighbours and friends, Elisabeth and Robert had turned many heads when they started dating in the mid 1990s. In the central Alberta town of Westlock, the Sand and Colbourne families shared plenty of good times. Backyard barbeques, hunting, camping, roasting marshmallows. Friends since early childhood, Robert and Elisabeth had gone through the "boys have cooties" stages, past the playful teasing and wet willies phase, into puberty, and then into each other's arms. It had seemed inevitable. And while their lives may have taken drastically different paths in recent years, their bond remained strong. But sometimes, like now, Elisabeth wondered how well she really knew Robert.

* * * * * *

Westlock is the kind of town you could blink and miss. An hour north of Edmonton, it is a pretty enough farming community, with colourful floral baskets dotting the wide, tar-patched streets, and small, lush lawns bursting with vegetable gardens. Homes are modest, although some on the north end of town sport two-car garages. Campers and trailers seem to fill every second driveway, a sign people are anxious to get out of town whenever possible. A large number of area lakes beckon many of the town's 4,800 residents, especially on the weekends. Everything seems big, from the expansive, wide-open skyline to the super-sized mosquitoes and grasshoppers which seem to have settled on Westlock as their permanent summer residence, snacking on nearby leafy farm fields.

There isn't a lot to do for those who call this place home, especially when you are young. It doesn't take long to tire of loitering around McDonalds, A&W, Subway, KFC and the two local grocery stores. Hooligan's Bar sounds like fun, but getting in underage is nearly impossible in a community where everyone knows everyone else. Thursday nights are hopping at the Hitching Post Saloon, where locals parade their worst impressions of Garth Brooks and Alan Jackson at the ever-popular karaoke night. Liquid courage is definitely a requirement before most take the stage.

With boredom comes trouble, and the Royal Canadian Mounted Police stationed in Westlock are kept busy, mostly with the sort of mischief crimes that teens tend to get into. The Towne Square, filled during the summer with potted plants and floral arrangements, is a popular place for local drunks and young ne'er-do-wells to relieve themselves and vandalize. Staff at the IGA and Extra Foods stores have their hands full keeping an eye on young shoplifters who seem to do it more for sport than necessity.

Drugs are rampant in the area, a dark underside that everyone seems to know about, but nobody wants to discuss. Marijuana is the drug of choice, much of it home-grown, courtesy of sparse farmland and isolated homes that make it easy to get away with. Being so close to Edmonton, it isn't difficult to get harder drugs into Westlock and the surrounding farm communities, which include Clyde, Thorhild, and Boyle. All the youth in the area seem to be doing it, most willingly, but some succumbing to the pressure of having an entire town thinking you're a wimp.

Cocaine first made its presence felt in the Westlock-area in the mid 1990s. A local resident, who had just turned 16 and received a souped-up truck, had gone into Edmonton, purchased a few rocks of crack, and brought them back to the community. A handful of local drugs users were eager to try something new, and they loved the results. In fact, they couldn't get enough, and soon were making their own two-hour return trips into the big city to stock up. The gang quickly learned how to purify their coke by mixing a spoonful of it in water and baking soda, heating the mixture to burn off the impurities, skimming the purified oil with a knife, waiting for the oil to solidify in to a rock, and then melting the rock into a bed of ashes, to be smoked in a pipe. Things quickly got out of hand as addiction began to take over.

Naturally, with drugs come crime, but the crime rate seems to fluctuate from month to month in Westlock, although not nearly as much as it used to. In the past, police never had to look far for the cause – if the Sand brothers were in jail, it usually meant quiet days and peaceful nights. But when they were out, God help everyone.

* * * * * *

Robert still carried a heavy heart over a tragic incident from August 1995, the kind of life-changing event which would stay with him forever. The Westlock summer fair was on, an annual event filled with carnival rides, games of chance and sweet, sticky and salty foods. Robert, his best friend Richard Ford, and several other friends went to a liquor store in town, where Richard was able to buy a six-pack of beer without being carded. He was only 16, but looked of age, thanks to his lanky build. One of the other friends had some pot. They all drove to an isolated spot in Westlock's Industrial Park, just on the edge of town, to drink, smoke joints and eat pizza. Suddenly, Richard began to cough uncontrollably. Everyone, especially Robert, knew he was in trouble. Richard, a severe asthmatic, had been hospitalized only weeks earlier for another serious attack. Richard began giving himself squirts from the inhaler, crying, sweating and foaming at the mouth. "I'm going to die," he gasped to his friends. He pleaded with them to get him to hospital.

The group arrived at the hospital within minutes, but had trouble getting inside, as the doors were locked. They frantically buzzed the intercom and kicked the doors, finally catching the attention of a nurse, who rushed Richard to the emergency room. Robert and the others paced nervously in the waiting area. They grew agitated when the nurse began questioning them about their drug and alcohol intake that night. Robert rushed past the nurse and stormed into Richard's hospital room, where he found his best friend in dire straits. His eyes were glazed, veins bulged in his neck, and doctors had several tubes feeding into his body. Richard began to defecate and urinate, and Robert was ordered out of the room in a scene of total chaos.

Robert couldn't take it. He felt guilty, and helpless. Hours later, doctors came into the waiting room with the grim news – Richard had gone into cardiac arrest and died. They tried everything to revive him, from CPR to adrenaline to electrical stimulation. The official cause of death was an asthma attack, likely brought on by the drugs and beer. Robert was devastated.

A pall bearer at his friend's funeral, Robert kept his emotions hidden from even those closest to him, rarely wanting to discuss Richard's death. He fell into despair, taking deadly risks with his own life like when, high on pot, he drove a friend's Mustang down the highway in the wrong lane of traffic.

Robert began spending more time with Sharon Ford, but rarely spoke directly about what happened to her son, Richard, whom he described as his only true friend. He also told Sharon he felt guilty he couldn't do more to help Richard, blaming it on the drugs he took. Robert was also simmering with anger at the way police had treated him. He had seen it too many times, with his own father and some of his friends. Robert soon began experimenting with harder drugs, like crack cocaine, which accelerated his freefall.

While camping in the woods one night, Robert woke up, violently screaming out Richard's name. His parents, Dennis and Elaine, were used to Robert's sleep-walking habits and used cold water to get him out of his trance-like state. Still, Robert refused to talk about Richard with his parents. But everyone could see something was horribly wrong. Inside, it was slowly eating away at Robert, his self-control seeping away.

* * * * * *

Elisabeth had always vowed to stand by Robert, although he could certainly test her commitment like no other. When he began going through the revolving door of the youth criminal justice system, still struggling with the pain of losing his best friend, Elisabeth remained by his side, the good girl with the bad boy. They were the ultimate odd couple. She had constantly pleaded with him to get his act together, stop being so selfish, but Robert, although ashamed to face her at times, could never go through with the many promises he had made.

Following several stormy months together, which seemed to stretch their lifelong friendship to the very limit, Elisabeth had made the mature decision to end it, promising to always remain loyal and loving, but from a safer distance. Robert hadn't fought her, although neither liked the outcome. Robert still wanted to run away together, to live in the woods, camp out like they had when they were kids, live off the land. Elisabeth was horrified about leaving her friends and family, but Robert joked they would make sure they were always near a pay phone.

"You can run down the hill and call your mom," he would say.

The feelings were definitely still there, for both of them, but Elisabeth had to fight them back with the reality of the situation. She told Robert things would have to change, in a big way, and Robert knew it. Now, after his latest stretch, he was finally out, and on the right track. Maybe lightning would strike twice.

As a young offender, Robert had managed to rack up 13 convictions, most resulting in probation or fines, which he rarely paid. But his biggest mistake came in April 1998, shortly after he had been freed from jail, making yet another vow to clean up his act, only to fail miserably. Robert, 19, was at a house party and wanted to get beer, but had no vehicle. No problem, he would just take one from someone else.

Robert, his then-girlfriend Sonja Boutin and a 15-year-old friend came up with a plan to order a pizza, then jump the delivery boy for his car when he arrived. They executed the plan perfectly, at least until they got into the car and it broke down. Robert and the other two set it on fire, then stole a truck at a nearby farm, which they later burned. They repeated the pattern of stealing and burning twice more, ending up some 300 kilometres south of Westlock in the town of Sylvan Lake. Days later, having turned much of the cash into drugs, Robert and another strung-out friend, Tom Fitzpatrick, decided to rob a small country grocery store. They put black nylon stockings over their heads, then burst into the Perryvale Country Store armed with a gun. Fitzpatrick grabbed the cash box, but was nervous and dropped it on the floor, spreading bills and coins everywhere. As this happened, the cashier's two-year-old son walked in from the back room, to see his Mommy being confronted by two masked gunmen. Robert's nerves were frazzled, but he remained calm, telling the woman to keep her cool so her son wouldn't be afraid. He and Fitzpatrick gathered up the cash, plus booze and cigarettes, then fled the store.

They continued their crime spree days later, when Robert and an underage teen friend burst into the Road House Tavern in the small town of Fawcett, armed again with a sawed-off .22 semi-automatic rifle and black nylons. The 15-year-old teen held the gun to the head of the store owner, while Robert grabbed $70 and six bottles of liquor. Robert and the teen fled, meeting up with some other friends at a nearby gravel pit to drink and celebrate. But the party would be short-lived.

Sonja's parents, who never did like the influence Robert had on their daughter, had tipped off the police, who tracked down the suspects and set up a spike belt on the highway. Robert was driving a stolen truck, his young companions at his side, when he came across a police dragnet the following morning and tried to speed away. Soon, he was driving down country roads, on just his rims, after three of the four tires were punctured by a road belt. A RCMP helicopter joined in the chase. The teen in the truck grabbed his gun, opened the rear window, and began shooting at a pursuing police car. He missed, and police began returning gunfire, knocking out Robert's last good tire. Another occupant grabbed the spare tire from inside the box of the truck, throwing it at the police car, along with several empty beer bottles. Robert eventually turned into a farmer's field, which proved to be a mistake. He smashed into a fence, and the police car was right on his tail, nailing his truck from behind. The boys tried to run, but were quickly caught.

The law had finally caught up to Robert big time, who was convicted in October 1998 of several charges, after his 15-year-old "friend" snitched to police about everyone's role. Robert had remained silent, but it ended up costing him. He was sentenced to seven years in prison, and at the age of 19, was facing the biggest challenge of his life. In prison at Drumheller, Robert initially felt sorry for himself. Sonja, the longest girlfriend of his life at two years, broke up with him, not wanting to wait for a convict boyfriend. But through it all, Elisabeth remained loyal, although deep down she wondered where things had gone so wrong.

* * * * * *

Elisabeth was especially close with Robert's younger brother, Danny. "Little Sis", he would call her, and she considered him a brother. Dusty, the youngest of the three Sand boys, was also a good friend. Danny and Dusty loved to pick on her when they were young, but Robert, her saviour, would always ride to the rescue, scolding his younger brothers for being so mean.

"She's just a little girl," he would say with a mischievous grin.

Robert only had two years on her, Danny one, and Dusty was the same age, but she still did seem little next to these brutes. Robert and Elisabeth could still spend hours laughing about the good times they shared growing up.

Unfortunately, Danny had taken a nosedive similar to his elder brother. At the age of 18, Danny thought he was in love and was even talking marriage, but his girlfriend abruptly broke up with him because her parents didn't approve of his less-than-stellar background. Danny went off the deep end, repeatedly phoning the girl and leaving frightening messages on her answering machine, threatening to harm her family. His cocaine use got heavier, and his crimes intensified. He viewed his past endeavours as lightweight. Danny told friends he wanted to be the meanest, toughest guy in town, the one everyone feared yet somehow admired at the same time. At five-foot-nine, he wasn't the biggest guy around, but he was certainly the most unpredictable. Danny began listening to hardcore death-metal music, distancing himself from his family and closest friends, all in the name of getting his next score. At the same time, he began burying himself in the Bible, memorizing scripture.

When Danny turned 18, he started hanging around Hooligan's Bar in Westlock, a gritty establishment filled with truckers on layovers, highway construction crews spending the night, local users and dealers, and even the occasional Hells Angel passing through town. One night, a group of college students from Edmonton, on a "pub crawl" through the area, stopped in for a drink, or ten. Darren Peacock, a long-time friend of Danny's, had just started working as a bouncer, a job the burly teen with a short-fuse seemed perfect for. He had spent countless days and nights with the Sand boys, doing drugs, shoplifting, getting drunk and acting stupid. But on this night, it was Danny who stole the show.

Two of the young men on the pub crawl approached Darren, who was working the door, and asked if he knew where they could find an eight-ball of coke. Darren knew there was no way in hell that much would ever just be laying around in town, so he walked over to Danny, who was downing beers in the bar with some friends. He told his buddy about the proposal.

"I've got a plan. Give me their money, and I'll go get an eight-ball for us. Then tell them you gave the money to somebody who promised to get you the coke, but they took off and ripped you off," Danny said with a wicked smile.

Darren was nervous about the idea, not wanting to stir up trouble, especially with strangers. But Danny assured him everything would be fine, and Darren trusted his friend. He'd seen Danny take care of himself in enough fights to feel safe. Danny jumped in a friend's car, made the return trip to Edmonton, and came back with the eight-ball. Sort of. Danny had smoked at least two-thirds of it by the time he returned. Darren, meanwhile, had to fend off the irate men who had given him the money. They began chasing him in the bar, but Darren's boss got in the middle, and kicked them out without further incident or retribution. Danny was high as a kite and feeling pretty good about himself.

* * * * * *

Robert and Danny, along with others in their small circle, spoke frequently about their hatred for police and authority. Police were what stood between them and the life they wanted to live, one filled with all the freedom they wanted and no rules. The police were the only ones saying no, and were the natural enemy because of it. "Hey, look, the fucking pigs" was a popular phrase to shout at the sight of a passing RCMP car.

Robert saw police as the enemy, demi-gods who loved flexing their muscles and flashing their badges. He saw them all as a big lie. He had watched his father stand up to police time after time, and he had vowed to never back down. As much as Robert despised the police, Danny's anger ran even deeper. There was really no reason for it, just a lack of respect for anyone who stood in his way of doing whatever he damn well pleased. Anarchy. It was what Robert and Danny began to believe in. They saw the world as a mess, and nobody seemed to be doing anything to fix it. "Maybe if we had total anarchy, then we could start all over again," Robert often said.

The small circle of friends, bored with life in the area and always looking for a new adventure, partied hard, gathering regularly in an abandoned house in Westlock, or meeting at night in the bush or local gravel and sand pits. Robert and Danny would sometimes light up the night, bringing a stolen vehicle to the party, then dousing it with gasoline and striking a match to use it for a bonfire. The tight-knit group of friends remained loyal to each other, acting as lookouts and accomplices when needed, offering alibis and cover-stories to the police. They came up with their own motto about life in the Westlock area – "Drinking, Fucking and Fighting".

* * * * * *

Danny was always struggling to find his place in the world, always trying to adapt. As a young boy, he would do outrageous things to get noticed, such as starting small fires. Danny was the most unpredictable of all the Sand boys. In grade two, he spent one recess running after cars, barking like a dog. There was no reason for this. It was just Danny being Danny. During his teens, he decorated his body with tattoos –

26

"Fearless, Painless, Senseless" across his stomach, "TCOB" across his knuckles (taking care of business), artwork all over his arms, and several smaller ones throughout his body. Danny experimented with his hair, regularly changing colours, styling it different, and even shaving a spider web into it one time. It was attention he craved, and there was never a shortage, it seemed.

Danny's first stint in youth jail came after a classmate called his brother, Dusty, a "pussy". Danny walked up to the boy and punched him right in the face, shattering his braces. "Don't bug my brother," is all Danny said.

But for all his faults, Danny did have a bizarre, Robin Hood-like sense of right and wrong. In his early teens, he was helping collect donations for Santa's Anonymous through his life-skills program. Danny suspected some of the local merchants carrying the festive donation boxes were stealing coins, and was wild with anger. He decided to set up his own "sting" operation, one which even veteran police officers would have admired. Using some of his own coins, Danny marked them and placed them inside the boxes, which he would empty out twice a week. Sure enough, he caught one store owner when he discovered his marked money out of the boxes and confronted the man, finding it in his possession. Danny was on top of the world.

"Wow, this kid is really sticking up for the poor!" the owner later told Danny's teacher.

In his late teens, Danny began speaking of grandiose plans for the future, such as becoming a drug kingpin in British Columbia or even joining the Hells Angels. He had met some bikers during previous stints in jail and had some inviting offers. Danny, once the class clown and life of the party, began to withdraw from society. During one stint in jail, he wrote a poem:

"It's a shame I spent so much of my life locked away on the inside, never expressing myself, instead letting everybody see the anger I unleashed, the pain I inflicted on so many innocent lives. I didn't pause my life a moment to notice Satan and his evil deeds ruined and ran down the realm of the world around us. But all we were thinking about was the next fix, the greater high, the evil sick twisted sins that were forced into our minds."

Danny's breaking point came in late 1999, more than a year after Robert had already been sent away for his crimes. Danny was driving with a friend, J.J. Martinkus, in the Westlock area. A car cut them off, and Danny, to nobody's surprise, wanted to confront the occupants. He followed them to a restaurant, waving a tire iron in their faces. He left without further violence, but the victims called police. Const. Curtis Davis, a Westlock RCMP officer, tracked Danny down, to speak to him about the road-rage incident. Danny responded by grabbing the officer's throat and punching him in the face. Several other officers fought hard to restrain Danny, eventually overpowering him. Danny became a local legend for the attack, which landed him in jail but cemented his reputation as a hot-head with no control.

Danny got out of jail in the spring of 2000 and went right back to cocaine. On June 5 of that year, Danny snapped, his hatred for police bubbling over. Const. Ron Gamble of the Edmonton Police Service was asked to respond to a suspicious vehicle call in the northeast part of the city. He arrived to find Danny Sand parked in a dark alley. Gamble got out of his car to investigate, but Danny, seeing another chance to stick it to the cops, threw his truck into drive and tried to run down Gamble, who jumped behind the cruiser car for safety. Danny smashed into the side, while Gamble drew his gun and fired, hitting Danny's back grill once.

Danny was convicted in May 2000 of dangerous driving and possession of stolen property, for which he was sentenced to two years, two days in prison. He was released from Drumheller in late September 2001, having been denied earlier bids for parole, but despite ongoing concerns from prison officials. "It seems the closer he gets to his statutory release date, the worse his attitude gets…he has made it clear that his attitude is one of a criminal who is unwilling to change," one official wrote.

"His problem was an inappropriate value system that obviously condones violence," wrote another.

Danny refused to speak with a prison psychologist, but officials had no choice – once he had served two-thirds of his time, he was a free man, thanks to federal legislation aimed more at rehabilitation than retribution. Upon his release, an overjoyed Danny told Elisabeth and Robert he was never going back.

"Ever since the first time I've been there, I hated it. It's the worst place in the world. It's for animals, and I'm not an animal," he said. He promised to go straight, and appeared to be succeeding.

Danny found a full-time job at the Edmonton Stockyards, a cattle auction market, where he was fixing fences and herding cattle. His pay quickly rose from $8 per hour to $8.65, and Danny loved the physical challenge of the job. He also found a roommate, Kevin Graham, a co-worker who he had bonded with. The pair loved to unwind at night by smoking pot together and discussing their future. Danny spoke about finding a woman to fall in love with, getting married and having lots of babies.

"This is it. I'm leading the straight and narrow path. I don't want to put you through the pain anymore, or my parents," Danny told Elisabeth upon his release.

She was glad to hear this, but concerned by the ultimatum at the end of their phone conversation – Danny said he would rather die then go back to prison.

"Danny, that's not going to happen," Elisabeth told him.

"Well, I'm telling you now just in case," he replied.

* * * * * *

With Danny on the outside looking in, Robert had been counting down the days until his own release, on November 1, 2001. He was anxious to finally be able to spend Christmas with his family and friends somewhere outside a tiny cement and steel room in Drumheller, with its ratty artificial Christmas trees, mistletoe and poor attempt at a festive environment. It had been almost three years to the day that Robert had gone in for the longest sentence of his life, and freedom couldn't come any quicker. But he had impressed prison officials, who first saw him as a bitter, violent young man. Robert had made the most of his time, enrolling in an anger management class, completing construction safety and petroleum industry service training courses, and finishing a cognitive skills program. He was even downgraded from medium to minimum security in the final months of his lengthy sentence.

"From this point of view, his progress has been exceptional," a caseworker wrote in the summer of 2001.

It had now been only a few weeks since Robert was released from Drumheller, and moved to Edmonton to live at the Stan Daniels Healing Centre. But it felt like a lifetime. He loathed being on a leash, having his every movement controlled and watched. He despised having to keep track of time. He had never needed a watch before, but now it was the difference between his freedom and a cage. While in jail, Robert grew angrier with each passing day, hating his life and vowing to never make the same mistakes again in trusting others and placing his life in their hands. Robert also hated being on parole, especially the rules he was told so often he had to follow, or else. He saw everyone around him as sheep, flocking to their jobs, their commitments, believing in everything, working for nothing. He knew what society demanded of him, and he didn't like it.

Christmas 2001 was going to be special, as it would be the first time in five years the Sand family would all be together. Dennis and Elaine Sand, along with Dusty, would always celebrate the holiday season, but it wasn't the same with Robert and Danny being stuck in Drumheller. This year, Elaine was going to make a turkey with all the trimmings, as both Danny and Robert would be able to come to Westlock. Dennis and Elaine left the house relatively bare, waiting for the boys to arrive so they could all decorate together, just like they had done years earlier.

Robert had got a taste of the family life weeks earlier, on Remembrance Day – his father's birthday. Dennis and Elaine had come to visit him at Stan Daniels, bringing a small cake they all shared, along with plenty of laughs. They had talked about the future, saying very little about the past. Elaine had even taken her son shopping for some new clothes, CDs and a cell phone, as Robert was looking for a job, anything to put some money in his pockets and some hope in his future. He found some odd jobs with a local temp agency, selling keychains door-to-door, collecting garbage, but didn't enjoy the work, fearing he would be stuck in these types of dead-end jobs the rest of his life.

Robert was also worried about his health. While nearing the end of his sentence, he had become convinced he had cancer. His lungs didn't feel right, his body was weak, and years of abuse at his own hands were taking their toll. Upon his release, Robert had gone to a doctor to have some tests run, but left before the results were back. Robert was convinced he was sick, and possibly dying.

As Christmas fast approached, Elisabeth's concerns about Robert were heightened. In the weeks leading up to his release, all Robert ever talked about was how he was going to make things right – with his family, and with Elisabeth. Robert had seemed to take the bull by the horns, not wanting to go back to the hellhole in Drumheller. But in their handful of day-time meetings since late November, when Robert would leave Stan Daniels and come to Elisabeth's apartment, he no longer seemed like the same person. Besides showing up late, he began complaining about work, felt he no longer had a rosy future, and seemed pre-occupied, distracted, and rarely spoke about his own plans for the future. Elisabeth worried the shine of his release had worn off, the lessons learned suddenly gone, and that trouble was ahead.

"I'm never going to amount to anything," he complained to Elisabeth during one of their increasingly infrequent telephone conversations.

One evening in early December, Elisabeth got a phone call. "Hey Little Sis," the caller said. It was Danny. The pair talked for a while, with Danny inviting Elisabeth over to his apartment, which was also in downtown Edmonton. Danny had mentioned Robert would be there, as Stan Daniels was letting him spend the evening with his brother. Elisabeth wanted to see the boys, but had an uneasy feeling in her stomach, as the visits with Robert were becoming more uncomfortable, almost to the point where she wondered if she really knew him anymore. But Elisabeth wasn't about to say no, especially to Danny. She pulled on her thick winter coat, braved the frigid night air, and made the quick trip over. Danny greeted her at the door, and let her in. Elisabeth stopped dead in her tracks. Sitting on the couch, beside Robert, was a ghost from the past.

CHAPTER TWO

They had met, by chance, their paths crossing outside the Edmonton Centre, a mega-shopping complex located in the heart of the city. Robert had been in a hurry, anxious to visit his good friend Elisabeth while on a day pass from the halfway house. It was a frigid morning, and Robert hadn't planned on making any pit stops as he scurried from the Edmonton facility towards Elisabeth's nearby apartment, where she surely would have a pot of hot coffee waiting. As he waited to cross mid-morning traffic, Robert's eyes were drawn to a troubled-looking girl standing at a bus stop. At first glance, she seemed like just another lost young soul, devoid of hope and seemingly unaware of the busy world which was passing by. Radical streaks of colour in her tangled hair drew a few curious stares, but Robert was struck by her shockingly thin frame, which was hardly protected from a harsh Prairie winter by a thin, ratty jacket. The girl turned and looked towards Robert, staring blankly. A chill went up Robert's spine. He knew this girl, yet hardly recognized her. It was Laurie Bell.

* * * * * *

…The sex had been great, maybe the best of their lives, the night Robert and Laurie were first introduced to each other at a wild and raucous house party in Westlock. It was 1998, just

months before Robert would be sent away to prison, and
19-year-old Robert couldn't take his eyes off the teen beauty
across the room. Full of life and energy, a devilish smile filling
her face, Robert had introduced himself to 16-year-old Laurie,
who also went by the name Tina. To many, Tina was just a
nickname. To Laurie, Tina was an alter-ego, the wild party-girl
who could let her hair down, get dirty and not worry about a
soul. To Robert, her name hadn't been all that important that
first night.

Robert and Laurie immediately hit it off. Laurie was from
Athabasca, about an hour north of Westlock, but she was
spending a lot of her time in the area these days. Problems at
home, or something like that. That was about as deep as the
conversation got that night, between shots of hard liquor, beer
and plenty of pot. Robert had a girlfriend, Sonja Boutin, but
they were having problems. It was an open relationship, at
least he viewed it that way, and besides, she had already
passed out. It wasn't long before Robert and Laurie snuck
away to an empty room inside the party house, got naked, had
a wild water fight with each other, then crawled under the
sheets, and gave each other a proper Westlock introduction.
Drinking, Fucking and Fighting, just like the saying goes...

* * * * * *

Three years had passed since their brief fling, and Robert
couldn't believe this was the same girl who now stood before
him. *What has happened to her,* he thought. He walked up to
Laurie, hoping she would remember him. Robert's dream of a
tearful, emotional reunion was dashed. Laurie did seem to
recognize him, but she could barely put two words together.
Her eyes were glazed, her skin ghostly pale. Robert knew the

signs, and knew she was either going up, or most likely given the time of the morning, still coming down. It broke his heart to see her like this. He hated to see drugs, especially hard ones like cocaine and speed, controlling someone. He wanted to hear Laurie laugh, see her smile, feel her kiss. But she was in horrible shape, and Robert knew he had to do something. He couldn't just leave her here, alone at a bus stop, at the mercy of the chemicals inside her fragile body. Robert knew he couldn't take her back to his "home", as they wouldn't allow him to bring a woman with him to the halfway house. Robert thought about Elisabeth, but felt it would be too awkward to bring Laurie there. Besides, he never liked mixing Elisabeth up in his problems, although he had failed on all levels in that department, a fact he would later regret. Robert knew his brother's apartment was also nearby. He grabbed Laurie by the hand, telling her he would take care of her, get her some place warm, a bed to sleep on, some clean clothes, whatever it took. Laurie didn't offer any resistance, and followed behind.

Kevin Graham returned home during the lunch hour to find two visitors inside his apartment. Robert was fine, a frequent guest to the bachelor pad he shared with Danny Sand. But the girl asleep on his couch had to go. Kevin prided himself on keeping a relatively clean home, and was doing his best to keep Danny in line, for Danny's own good. He knew all about Robert's past, and didn't want to see one Sand boy drag the other down. Kevin could see the girl on the couch was a wreck, and he wasn't buying Robert's explanation that he just needed to help her out, that he knew her from back home and felt obliged to help her. Kevin said they'd have to find someone else to freeload off, and Danny, who had also come home, didn't put up an argument. Robert grudgingly agreed, and woke Laurie up. He explained the situation, and she was now

37

clear-headed enough to make a few phone calls. She quickly found a friend, in the west-end, who would take her in. Robert was relieved, although still puzzled and concerned. Kevin offered to drive her to a nearby convenience store, where Laurie would be picked up. She promised to stay in touch with Robert, who told her about his new residence at Stan Daniels. Robert left, headed to Elisabeth's, hours late and unsure of what to say to his good friend.

* * * * * *

Several days passed, and Robert had still put off telling Elisabeth what was on his mind. He knew she was suspicious, but didn't want to get into it with her, especially about Laurie. When speaking with Elisabeth, he told her he was just having a "shitty week", and not to worry about him. But Robert realized he couldn't keep Laurie away from Elisabeth forever. Their paths would collide soon enough.

On a frosty early December morning, Laurie went to Stan Daniels to meet with Robert. Once again, she was high as a kite, oblivious to the world and in obvious despair. Laurie said it was Valium, and Robert began lecturing her, knowing his words were likely falling on deaf ears. He made a vow, to take Laurie under his wings, help her make a clean start of things, then take her back to her family in Athabasca. In no time at all, this had become his mission. It started to consume him.

Robert began focusing his entire life on Laurie, leaving Stan Daniels at every opportunity and spending all his free time with her, hoping to keep her off the drugs and away from the bad influences which had obviously taken hold of her. He began to see positive results, almost immediately. The colour was coming back to Laurie's skin, she was more coherent, she regained an appetite and was even able to share some laughs with Robert, something which hadn't seemed possible only days earlier. But those closest to Robert weren't laughing. Elisabeth was worried sick about him, as his phone calls and visits were quickly phased out. It took a handful of voice mail messages at Stan Daniels before Robert even returned her call during the second week of December.

"What's wrong?" Robert asked, in a voice which suggested he was in a hurry and didn't have much time to talk to a woman he could usually spend hours, if not days, talking to about nothing in particular.

"Lots of things are wrong, Rob. You're acting really weird," Elisabeth said.

Robert said life was all mixed up. Elisabeth, sensing a slip-up was inevitable, encouraged Robert to stay focused on his own life, and not worry about anyone else.

"Five more months you have to live in the halfway house. It's not that bad," she said.

Robert agreed, but Elisabeth didn't believe him for a second. She feared Robert was a runaway train, bound to go off track at any time.

Her worst fears were confirmed during the chance meeting at Danny's apartment. Elisabeth walked in to find Robert on the couch, Laurie sitting next to him, looking in bad shape. Elisabeth knew about their history, and always thought Laurie wasn't good enough for Robert. She hadn't seen Laurie in several years, and was shocked at her changed appearance.

"What the hell are you doing?" Elisabeth demanded of Robert. He struggled to find the words to answer.

"I want to help her. I want to clean her up, get her off drugs. I can't leave her on the street," Robert said, barely able to make eye contact with Elisabeth.

* * * * * *

Athabasca. Located on the banks of the historic Athabasca River, the 3,000 residents who call this north-central Alberta town home can always count on a refreshing breeze off the water to cool even the hottest of summer days. Aboriginals first travelled the 1,232 kilometre waterway through Athabasca by birch bark canoe, replaced later by fur traders in canoes, then York boats. The Hudson's Bay Company relied on the route to move goods through the province, connecting the north and south with each other. Beneath a massive "Keep Alberta Green – Help Prevent Forest Fires" sign which sits on a cliff overlooking the river, pointing directly at Main Street and welcoming visitors, is a large monument celebrating the town's rich history and connection to the river.

But beneath the town's shiny surface lurks a dark, and dirty secret. Drug use is rampant, much like its neighbours to the south in Westlock, Clyde, Thorhild and Boyle, but perhaps less hidden and subtle. Locals describe teens as young as 12 walking around town like "zombies". Speed, or "jib" to many users, is the town favourite, replacing marijuana and ushering in a frightening new reality. In the summer of 2003, a young man committed suicide. Townsfolk say it was over a drug debt he couldn't handle. Like many rural Prairie communities, there just isn't much to do when you're young. A message scratched out on a park bench, located in a picturesque park along the riverfront, seems to sum up the mood of the community's youth. *"Potheads are not criminals. Fuckin' catch the crack heads."*

For years, Laurie had resisted the temptation, refused to give in, thanks largely to the positive role model in her life – her mother, Donna Bell. Donna was still in her teens when she got pregnant with her first child, Andrea. Two other girls quickly followed – Lynn, then Laurie. A registered nurse working a full-time job at a town doctor's office, Donna was basically a one-woman show, as her husband, Neil, offered little support. The couple divorced when Laurie was nine, but the relationship had ended years earlier. A heavy drinker, Neil never seemed able to keep a job for long. He would toil away at odds and ends, although he enjoyed his time driving truck and hauling hay to the United States. Neil's favourite hangout was the Union Hotel, a 91-year-old establishment which would be best described by those who frequented it as having "character". Behind the bar, a small sign welcomes visitors to the "Union Hotel, where good friends meet". Some not so good friends, as well, judging by the "barred" list posted on the wall, listing 24 different people, mostly men but, surprisingly, a handful of women. Six others names are on the list as being under the age of 18 and not allowed to drink. The lobby of the bar was as far as most Athabasca teens could get, and many of them would whittle away the hours there, begging for cigarettes, money, even free drinks. Occasionally, one of the regulars would slip a shot or two outside, but most of the time the youths were left sipping diet Coke and tap water.

* * * * * *

It would be difficult to find a woman who worked harder for her children than Donna Bell. And the Bell girls paid their mother back by staying out of trouble and getting reasonably good grades at Landing Trail Intermediate School, where teachers very rarely had problems with any of them. Unfortunately, Donna's job – which often included shift work – took her away from the girls more than she'd like, leaving the pre-teen girls without a full-time parent during some of the most crucial years of their lives. Laurie was seen by most as a quiet, shy and co-operative girl who knew how to have fun, but could also focus on serious projects and issues. She was a talented athlete, like her sisters, running track and playing various school sports. Most of the boys took a liking to Laurie, who was petite and pretty. But by the time Laurie reached Eden Parr High School, she had grown tired of being the same old predictable Laurie, and yearned for new experiences and adventures.

In her early teens, Laurie got an unexpected taste of big city life when she began hanging out with a girl, about her age, who talked frequently about getting out of Athabasca and finding adventure in Edmonton. Laurie listened with open ears as Amanda told her stories of wild parties filled with exciting people and an endless flow of booze and drugs. Laurie would often complain to her friends, in fact anyone who would listen, about being bored with Athabasca. There were hardly any parties in town, and most of her friends seemed so stale compared to the ones Amanda was talking about. It wasn't long before Laurie began looking beyond Athabasca.

One night, Laurie had a major meltdown when Donna caught her trying to sneak off to a party in Westlock. Frustrated by the changes in her teen daughter, Donna took the drastic step of calling Social Services, who came out to speak with Laurie. She was irate that her mother felt she needed professional help, and responded by scratching up her wrists, saying she didn't care if she lived or died.

Laurie began to drink, and, inevitably, turned to crime to help pay for booze. She would often shoplift, figuring it was the easiest way to make money, but Laurie wasn't very good. Local merchants began to catch her, and wondered what was happening to the sweet little Laurie they all knew. Donna was at her wit's end, juggling work and a chaotic home life, and sent Laurie to a group home for several months, figuring it would straighten her out. But all it did was give Laurie a taste of life outside the home, something she began to crave. Soon, Laurie was frequently running away, spending much of her time in Westlock with a young man she'd met at a party and quickly bonded with, Darren Peacock. In grade nine, she dropped out of school, her marks already having hit rock-bottom due to poor attendance and attitude. She seemed completely lost.

* * * * * *

She may have been small, but Laurie sure packed a wallop. Darren learned this the hard way, during the impromptu wrestling matches he would have with the wild, 95-pound spit-fire he quickly grew to love. Outside the family home, Laurie was free as a bird, and she loved to spread her wings. Speaking about family was considered taboo. Their play fighting would sometimes last for hours, stopping only to puff a joint or down a drink or two. And could Laurie ever drink. Her favourite was lemon gin, or "panty remover" as everyone called it. Darren and Laurie loved to have drinking contests, to see who could handle more. Usually Laurie won, despite Darren's large girth. But sometimes, they would both be the losers. One night in Westlock, a drinking binge came to an abrupt end when Laurie said she had to puke. The same urge came over Darren. Both rushed to the bathroom, arriving at the toilet at the same time. Laurie took the left side, Darren the right. Laurie was the first to hurl, which, of course, brought out the worst in Darren. Back and forth they went, seemingly forever, until the room reeked and their guts ached.

To sober up, Darren and Laurie learned to love coffee. They could find the bottom of a bottomless cup, spending hours in Westlock planning out future parties and social events. Darren loved to make Laurie laugh, and would do his version of stupid human tricks to get a roar every time. Laurie didn't know anyone else who could stick 70 French fries up his nose, or put his entire mouth around a large glass. Sure, it was stupid. But it was damn funny to see. They would sleep on friends' couches, basement floors, wherever, as long as it meant not having to be home. They called it "couch surfing". Darren and Laurie even broke into an abandoned Westlock home one night, where they filled a bowl with gasoline and struck a match, for light and heat. In their drunken and drug-induced stupour, the bowl tipped over, setting fire to the carpet.

Darren and Laurie would regularly shoplift together, with Darren as teacher and Laurie the student. Chocolate bars, make-up and hair dye became Laurie's specialities. At age 15, Laurie's girl-next-door appearance began to fade. She was using speed, which was introduced to the area by one of their friends who had gone to Edmonton. Laurie became hooked, craving her next hit, never satisfied with what she had. Her teeth began turning an ugly, tar-like black, and sleep was no longer a priority. Her hair was greasy, her clothes dirty.

Laurie began dating one of Darren's friends, Chad Cornwell, a local punk rocker. Laurie fell hard. It was her first major relationship, and it was filled with passion and intensity. Laurie and Chad couldn't keep their hands off each other, even if they were in front of Darren. The sex became risqué, with both wanting to try new things – it didn't matter where they were, whether it be outdoors, or in front of others. One day it was on a tractor, the next it would be in a public park. The relationship ended less than two years later, just as passionately as it began. Laurie's lifestyle caught up to her, and she began sleeping around on Chad, who found out about her infidelity. One of her partners was Robert Sand. Laurie and Chad argued, and Laurie decided to end it. Rather than tell Chad herself, she told a local tough in the Westlock area that Chad had beaten her. The man, who had ties to outlaw motorcycle gangs, paid Chad a visit.

"I'll teach him what it's like to be a bitch," the man said.

As a drug addiction began to take hold of Laurie, her behaviour became more erratic. Darren began spending less and less time with her, his life on a far more positive path, one filled with family, stable friends, school and work. Eventually, they lost all contact.

Laurie would occasionally return home to Athabasca, but would rarely go visit her mother or sisters. Instead, she'd go the Union Hotel, which she knew as more than just a hangout. For a few years in her mid-teens, it became a second home. Her father had taken refuge in the hotel, living in a small, one-bedroom suite above the bar. Laurie felt a certain connection with her father, who didn't worry about enforcing rules, or pestering her about what time she came home, who she was hanging out with and how she was doing in school. Laurie could just be herself, hang out, share some laughs, kick back and relax. Neil always treated his daughter well when she came to visit, giving up his bed so she could have a good night's sleep while he crashed on the living room couch. Laurie showed her love to her father through drawings, which decorated his suite. She wasn't going to win any awards, but Laurie's sketches were worth a million bucks to Neil. One of his prized possessions was a figure of a beautiful woman, with wings, and the caption "Love You, Dad" underneath. Laurie was indeed an angel to Neil.

* * * * * *

As she entered her late teens, Laurie started making trips to Edmonton with Amanda, who had found lucrative work as a hooker. Laurie didn't believe in selling her body for sex, but began hanging with a seedy crowd. She lived with her friend, who was also dancing at an amateur strip club called "Rookies". Laurie's fall from grace accelerated, her nights often filled with a hazy cloud of pot, speed, crystal meth and prescription pills, anything she could get her hands on. She grew even more distant from her family, and partied with death metal bands in Edmonton. One of her favourites, Dead Jesus, was known for bringing dead mice and pig guts on stage, and slashing their wrists during performances. Laurie, the groupie, loved the raw, hard-core scene, and would follow the band from gig to gig.

In the spring of 2000, Laurie met a new love, Gary Buzzell. Like her previous relationships, she jumped in with both feet. The pair shared a common love of partying at rave clubs such as Therapy and Climax in the city's gritty core. Both were addicted to drugs, which seemed to affect the status of their relationship on an hourly basis. Within weeks, Gary proposed and, of course, Laurie instantly accepted. But marriage plans were put on hold when Gary was arrested for theft and sent to Fort Saskatchewan jail.

Nearly two years after Darren had last seen Laurie, he ran into her in downtown Edmonton in the summer of 2001. Darren had managed to straighten out, moving away from his troubled past in Westlock, finding a home in Edmonton, a steady job and girlfriend. Darren was saddened to see Laurie had fallen even deeper into despair. She looked like she had just stumbled out of an all-night rave, complete with plastic beads all over her body, pacifier hanging from her neck (to avoid swallowing one's tongue during a drug-induced frenzy), bizarre rings on her fingers. She was frail, and large bags were under her eyes.

"What are you doing?" an incredulous Darren asked his one-time friend.

Laurie tried to respond, but couldn't form the words. Instead, she appeared to be chewing her tongue, saying something which sounded like "nam, num, nam". Darren walked away, shaking his head. It was only a few months later that Laurie, in a similar state, ran into her old flame, Robert Sand.

CHAPTER THREE

Dennis Strongquill was pacing the hallways of Yorkton Regional Hospital, trying to keep a grip on his nerves. Just a few metres away, his girlfriend, Mandy Delorande, lay flat on her back. Her blonde hair was pulled back tight, and beads of sweat dotted her face. Dennis could see she was in pain, and it was killing him.

"Just give her a caesarean," Dennis snapped at the nurse who had popped into the room.

For Mandy, the agony of childbirth was tolerable, almost routine. At 27 years of age, she had already gone through this four times, the first when she was only 16. But Dennis was a different story. He was 52, long past the typical age of dirty diapers and late-night feedings. The births of his first five children were a distant memory, the last coming seven years ago. He never remembered it being this difficult.

In the months leading up to November 2001, Dennis and Mandy had spent many hours picking out baby names, Mandy pulling for a girl and Dennis rooting for a boy. They had agreed to name a son Dennis Gregory, which filled Dennis with pride, the thought of a boy bearing his name. Mandy had dibs on the name if it was a girl – Korrie McKayla.

Dennis and Mandy had first gone to the hospital in Swan River, Manitoba, when she began having contractions on Halloween night. Mandy had checked into a room, and Dennis figured it would only be a matter of hours. Three days later, and still no baby. Now, they were in a different hospital, in a different town, in a different province. Doctors in Swan River thought a shift to Yorkton, Saskatchewan, just a couple hours west, would be best for what was turning out to be a long and gruelling labour. Just like Dennis, the baby was proving to be stubborn.

It was late in the day on November 2 when a groggy Mandy opened her eyes, struggling to get her bearings. Hours earlier, doctors had heeded Dennis's demands and agreed to put an end to the marathon by opening her up. Her final memory before drifting off to sleep had been of Dennis, decked out a pale blue hospital gown, smiling down at her, giving her a kiss on the forehead, and telling her "I love you". That was all she needed to feel safe, and secure. Her big, strong policeman was going to make sure everything was all right.

* * * * * *

Mandy scanned the room, desperate to see Dennis and the baby. Was it a boy, or a girl? In the corner, she saw Dennis standing, cradling a tiny, precious package in his arms.

"We have a girl. Say hi to Korrie McKayla," said Dennis, tears welling up in his eyes. Little Korrie was a spitting image of him, with her dark skin, black hair, and rosy, chubby cheeks.

Suddenly, the pain in her body was gone. Mandy just needed to look in Dennis's eyes, to see his joy, to know that everything was right in their world.

Dennis always loved children, to see them smile, hear them laugh. Nobody could brighten a child's day quite like Dennis. His favourite approach was the guitar, which could turn any little gathering into a grand old sing-song, with Dennis always leading the way. His children, and four grandchildren, loved to hear Dennis belt out a tune, usually one he'd make up off the top of his head, sounding like it would fit nicely on any scratchy old country music record. He would also lead children around in a mock march, shouting "one…two… three…four…one…two…three…four" in a rhythmic chant, his arms flapping wildly at his side.

Dennis initially battled mixed feelings about becoming a father again, at an age where he was already talking about retirement. He had just received his 20-year medal as a constable with the Royal Canadian Mounted Police, and had been thinking about retiring in a few years to live in a small, quiet cabin in the isolated Manitoba community of Barrows, where he'd spent much of his childhood. Dennis didn't have big dreams, didn't want to travel and see the world. A good book, a roaring fire, a guitar and a baseball glove, on the part of Earth he held so dear was the perfect way to enter his golden years. That would be Heaven to Dennis.

But everything had changed so quickly when Mandy gave him the news in early 2001. Their relationship, which had only began a year earlier and was still in a state of flux, had produced a child. Suddenly, Dennis felt like he was starting over again, at a time when he was supposed to be winding down. There were new responsibilities, ones he never thought possible just months earlier. He was going from a divorced bachelor to an expectant father with a young woman he was quickly developing feelings for. There would be a new family to support, love and protect.

Dennis had never doubted the love he had for Mandy, who had been a rock for him for many years. Twice-divorced, Dennis had become a shell of his former self following his most recent marriage – drinking heavily, battling depression, and taking life for granted. Mandy, who he'd known since she was a teen living in Barrows, had helped him through one of the toughest periods of his life. He loved her youth, her energy for life, and her passion for him. Mandy could make Dennis blush on demand, like the time he was playing in a fun slo-pitch baseball game and she got him to "focus" by cracking a sex joke. "Just think of num nums when you're up there," she said with a sly smile. Dennis turned 100 shades of red, but none of his teammates were any wiser.

Mandy also knew a thing or two about abuse, having fought through drug and alcohol addictions years earlier. She hadn't always been there for her children, the product of several failed relationships. But something changed for both of them when they got together in 2000. Each was given a newfound source of strength, a confidence that could only come from being together.

* * * * * *

With the baby on the way, Dennis had even began thinking about his own mortality. He knew policing had its risks – he had seen that first hand more than 15 years earlier when a fellow cop was killed on duty while they worked in the same rural Manitoba detachment. Dennis had been asleep when he heard Rob Thomas had been shot dead in Powerview, but he was never able to get the tragedy out of his head. No stranger to alcohol, Dennis hit the bottle even harder after Rob died.

Dennis used the killing as a basis to lecture his fellow officers about always keeping their eyes open, never taking anything for granted, and always protecting themselves and their partners.

"I know what can happen on the job. Don't goof around," he would often say.

Dennis worried about his own safety, but his biggest fear came from his own body. Dennis had a big heart, but it had taken a pounding thanks to years of eating, drinking and living the wrong way. Two minor heart attacks in recent years had given him quite a scare. He knew losing 20 pounds wouldn't kill him, but gaining 20 might. He had seen too many pairs of pants, too many belt buckles, get tossed in the back of the closet and exchanged for something a little bigger, a little looser.

In the summer of 2001, Dennis told Mandy he wanted to be buried at the Whispering Pines Cemetery in Barrows, a tiny memorial cut out of the deep bush and beneath a spacious sky. Mandy, who had no problem being involved with a man nearly twice her age, bristled at talk of Dennis's death. Dennis had even showed her the spot where he wished to be buried, a large plot beneath a towering pine tree. Dennis said he wanted to be at the back of the cemetery, so he could watch over everybody.

* * * * * *

Barrows is a small town, population around 200 on any given week, mostly elderly and middle-aged residents living in small, trailer-style homes. Located about 450 kilometres northwest of Winnipeg, survival means living off the land to a degree, and working rugged jobs like fishing, hunting and trapping. There is no gas station, no grocery store, no restaurant. For those amenities, locals must take the 45-minute drive south to Swan River – "going into town". Some residents don't even have phones, although many have satellite dishes, likely to stave off the boredom. For entertainment, there are few options. The Barrows Community Hall, besides feeding residents with a steady diet of Bingo, comes alive a few times each year, usually for a birthday party, anniversary or, the annual New Year's Eve dance, where everyone throws on their finest evening wear and comes out for a night to remember.

The fire hall, staffed by local volunteers, sits next door to the hall, but is rarely used or needed, thankfully. Just across the gravel road sits a poorly maintained baseball field, which has clearly seen better days. Overgrown with thick weeds and large ant hills, the lack of children in the area is revealed. Next to the baseball field sits an equally rundown hockey rink, the wooden boards rotted and rickety.

Dennis's first true love was sports, and as a child spent many nights listening to Montreal Canadiens games on the radio, and his passion for the Habs never waned. Whenever they were playing on television, Dennis could usually be found in his red and white Montreal jersey. He was equally fond of the Montreal Expos, and loved to spend a lazy afternoon watching a ball game on TV.

Dennis had been abandoned by his parents at a Powwow when he was only a few weeks old after having been born in northern Saskatchewan. The Genaille family took him, adopting him and raising him in a loving environment at Red Deer Lake, just north of Barrows on the extreme northwestern edge of Manitoba. A happy-go-lucky child, Dennis loved to make people around him happy. He always had a joke, or a wisecrack, for anyone within earshot. He became an elite athlete, at least in the eyes of the Barrows community, excelling in baseball and hockey. Dennis also loved to cook, and would often throw together his homemade macaroni soup, which was a palatable combination of noodles, wieners and tomatoes.

Dennis was known as a ladies man, a reputation he carried with him since birth, when his family gave him the nickname "Bosom". In fact, some in the community *only* knew him by that name, and would have given you a strange look if you asked about Dennis. As a child, Dennis always seemed to take a shine to a woman's chest, in particular burying his head in one. Dennis's friends and family joked that he never really did grow out of his habit.

Beneath the laughter and the smiles was plenty of pain. Dennis rarely spoke about his birth parents, yet began searching for his mother when he was about 30 years old. He found her, and learned she gave him up as a baby for fear her boyfriend – not his father – would kill her. It was a painful reunion, but developed into a cordial relationship making up for lost time. It ended suddenly when his mother died of complications from diabetes. Dennis had already lost several other adoptive relatives and close friends, as death and tragedy always seemed to be lurking just around the corner.

His first marriage, to Collette Aubin, had ended with an amicable split a decade earlier, following 18 years together. The couple had three children – Teresa in 1972, Joey in 1974 and Ricky in 1981. The pair remained friends following the split, which they chalked up to personality clashes and different outlooks on life.

His second marriage, to Donna Strongquill, was much shorter, ending soon after the birth of two children – Rachel in 1993 and Raven in 1994 – and countless arguments and fights. Much of the blame was accepted by Dennis, who had taken what was good in his life and drowned it in alcohol, briefly becoming a person that neither he nor others like very much. Donna had tried to help him, but was told at Alcoholics Anonymous meetings she was an "enabler" who was getting in the way of Dennis really confronting his problem by offering him a safe, comforting environment to continue drinking. The pair finally split in 1997 but never divorced. They remained friends to this day, although Dennis knew he'd have to one day make the separation legal though the courts, especially with Mandy such an important part of his life now. Dennis hit the bottle even harder following his break-up with Donna, but took his last sip in 1998, thanks to the help of his family, friends, and Mandy.

* * * * * *

Dennis first dreamed of being a police officer while watching a parade in Swan River, when he was just eight-years-old. As the colourful floats and mascots went by, waving to the children, one particular entry caught his eyes. The Royal Canadian Mounted Police, decked out in their crisp red serge, black pants and boots, left Dennis talking for days.

"I want to be a police officer when I grow up," Dennis told his family afterwards. Most people chalked it up to childhood ambitions which would never get fulfilled. But Dennis wasn't one to let his dreams die.

Earl Bement, a one-time hobo and train hopper who became a three-time mayor of Barrows, remembers the conversation like it just happened yesterday. Considering it was nearly 25 years ago, and Bement is now 87-years-old, the feat is even more impressive. He was mowing his lawn, being careful not to run over any large rocks, when the police pulled up to his house. Bement was curious, as his wife had told him they'd come by earlier, but didn't say what they wanted.

"I didn't do it. I was a mile away from here and I can prove it," said Bement, never one to miss the opportunity to crack a joke. The two officers smiled, and said they were actually there to get Bement's opinion. Seems a young boy named Dennis Strongquill had applied to be the first-ever band constable in Barrows. Bement, as mayor, had lobbied hard for a full-time officer for the area, who would offset the absence of a regular RCMP presence in the community. Bement didn't hesitate to answer.

"Dennis is a good, steady, straightforward, hardworking boy. If he gets the job as a constable, he would straighten this area out completely," said Bement.

Bement had known Dennis practically from birth, and meant every word he said. When Dennis was 17, he turned in to Bement a wallet he had found containing $60. Money was tight for everyone in the area, including Dennis and his family, and such a find would go a long way. But Dennis didn't waste any time doing the right thing. Now, years later, the area was being hit hard by vandals, drunks, and nuisance crimes, and Bement knew Dennis wouldn't stand for it. Days later, Dennis was hired.

As band constable, Dennis was responsible for maintaining law and order in Barrows, but also the nearby communities of Red Deer Lake, National Mills, Westgate and Powell. It was a tough job, and took a heavy toll on young Dennis, who came to Bement's home one day, about six months after he began the job.

"I haven't got any friends anymore," Dennis complained. He was getting all sorts of grief from former friends and neighbours, who didn't like the fact he had become a cop.

"Bosom, you don't have to worry about the friends you haven't got. They'll come around and realize what you're doing is for their benefit, as well as everybody else's," said Bement, sitting on the hood of his car.

Months later, Dennis came back, this time with a more positive outlook.

"Earl, I've just been offered a position in the Mounted Police. Should I take it?" asked Dennis.

"I'll break your head if you don't," Bement said with the straightest face he could muster.

Dennis never looked back, blazing a trail through the RCMP. One of his favourite moments had come in 1988, when he was briefly relocated to Calgary to work at the Winter Olympics. It was a sportsman's dream come true. Dennis made stops all over Manitoba, beginning in Churchill and ending most recently with his posting in early 2001 at the new detachment in Waywayseecappo. He had been given a choice of detachments to move to, and wanted to work on the native reserve, where he felt he could be a role model for young Aboriginals. There, he was posted with three other members, all Aboriginal, who quickly formed a strong bond. They were welcomed with open arms by the community, and Dennis was especially liked, a big teddy bear who always had time to talk, or a joke to tell.

Dennis loved the uniform, and would often wear it around Barrows, where he would stand out. He loved showing off his badge, which bore the number 40120. He took playful ribbing for it, especially when he went to official town functions like a dance at the community hall.

"Are you happy to be a god-damned lousy cop," Bement once joked with Dennis.

"Earl, if I knew you meant that, I'd get you," Dennis replied with a hearty laugh.

* * * * * *

Back in the hospital room in Yorkton, Dennis had a tight grip on little Korrie, while Mandy sat in the bed nearby, revelling in the afterglow. Dennis was carefully counting her tiny toes and fingers, making sure they were all there. He gave his daughter frequent kisses, making sure to rub his scratchy moustache on her little face, which seemed to get a reaction out of her. A nurse, who had been in the room, said she wanted to take Korrie away for a few minutes, just to clean her up, take some measurements and make sure everything was alright.

"Leave me alone for awhile. Come back later," Dennis told the woman, not even looking up from the beautiful sight in front of him. "I haven't felt so happy for a long while."

CHAPTER FOUR

Robert was running out of patience. He was tired of being told what to do and sick of always having to account for his time. Laurie needed him, more then just the few hours each day he could get away from the halfway house to see her. Besides, he couldn't be there when she needed him most – at night, when most people went to sleep but she came alive, hungry for her next fix. The house rules at Stan Daniels required him to check in by 10:30 p.m. or risk going back to jail.

In the days they had spent together, Laurie was showing real progress, and Robert was going to bed each night with a sense of self-satisfaction he hadn't felt in years, maybe ever. For once, he was doing something for someone else, not just himself. Robert wished he could explain this to the people in charge of his parole, to tell them he needed more time to help a friend, but he knew they wouldn't understand. They never did.

On December 10, 2001, things began to unravel in an awful hurry. Daytime had given way to darkness, and Robert and Laurie were together, drinking coffee and talking. Robert was glancing at the clock on the restaurant wall, knowing he was going to cut it close. They were making real progress this night, with Laurie opening up about her problems and fears, Robert holding her tightly, making her feel warm and safe.

They spoke about their friends, life experiences, lost love and hopes for the future. It was a perfect fit, for both of them, and neither wanted to let go. So they didn't, at least not for several hours.

Robert was fighting a mixture of emotions, knowing any screw-ups could ruin the special Christmas his family so desperately wanted, and needed. But there were other things to think about, and with Laurie in his arms, nothing else seemed to matter. Laurie mentioned she was in some trouble, that the police had charged her with shoplifting and that she was supposed to have been in court earlier in the day. She hadn't gone, not wanting to face the past, but her decision had created more problems for herself in the process. None of that mattered, though, because she was thinking about the future, with Robert. Once again, she was falling hard, and fast. Robert's strong, sinewy body swallowed her tiny frame, and she felt no worries when she was with him.

Robert spoke about his hatred of parole, how *they* were taking him away from her. The couple began discussing ways to fix their problems, to make everything right. Running away was one possibility, a chance to make a clean break, leave all the problems behind and start a new life, together. Yes, Christmas was coming and Robert knew he would disappoint his family, but he hoped they would see the good in what he was doing, understand that it was the right thing to do. Robert and Laurie, their minds racing, finally parted ways, their bodies unable to take any more caffeine, with a long hug and even longer kiss – Laurie clean and sober, Robert feeling a sense of pride.

As he walked back towards Stan Daniels, aware he was long overdue but still not showing any hurry, he was struggling to sort out the feelings in his heart, and head, towards Laurie.

Was this just lust, like it had been three years ago when he and Laurie met at the house party in Westlock? They'd had a good romp, shared some laughs, then parted ways – no promises, no commitments, just good, dirty fun. There were no strings attached, and Robert had wanted it that way. But did he now? Things seemed so different, sex wasn't important now. In just the few short days they'd been together, it seemed as if his whole world had changed.

* * * * * *

When he finally arrived back at the home, the fallout was immediate. Grounded by the living unit staff for missing curfew, Robert wouldn't be going anywhere until further notice. Granted, it could have been worse – at least they didn't call the cops and have him arrested. But when the new day arrived, Robert didn't see any light in the situation. Staff at the centre told Robert the they would lift his grounding and give him one more chance, but then pulled the plug hours later when they learned he'd used several bus passes in recent days. They felt he was abusing his privileges. He wanted to see Laurie, needed to see her, immediately. Robert worried what might happen to Laurie if he wasn't around, even if it was just one day. He was giving serious thought to leaving.

It was midday when Elisabeth called, worried because she hadn't spoken with Robert in several days. The anger in Robert's voice was evident – but Elisabeth sensed something else was going on inside the Robert, who she felt was slowly slipping out of her life.

"You don't sound very good," Elisabeth said, the conversation becoming awkward right off the bat. It never used to be hard to speak with Robert, but he was now so distant, so isolated, she never knew quite how to approach things.

"I'm pissed because they won't let me out today," Robert said.

Elisabeth told Robert not to do anything stupid, but feared the advice was too late. Robert said things had changed, his life was going in a new direction, one that may not include her. It was difficult for Elisabeth to hear, but certainly not unexpected. Robert didn't want to stay on the phone, but told Elisabeth he would explain everything in a letter he planned to write.

Robert had someone else he wanted to speak with, and Danny was at home when he called. Robert told his brother he was thinking of running away, with Laurie. He was tired of the rules, the hassles, and having to answer to authority.

"Don't do it," Danny said. But Robert hadn't really called for his brother's advice, and his mind was all but made up. Danny's pleadings would have no impact.

* * * * * *

A large, strapping man with a big strong hands, a comb-over and a few missing teeth, Dennis Sand looks like man who has gone a few rounds in his life, taking some shots but dishing plenty out as well. The 49-year-old used, and abused, alcohol, often in front of his three boys – Robert, Danny and Dusty – when they were young. A beer gut told tales of wasted nights and opportunities. And he was no stranger to police.

Dennis quit school in grade 10, when he began straying towards a life of petty crime. He briefly spent time in jail for a series of break-and-enters, and never backed down from a fight, even starting some of his own. Dennis often masked his faults with alcohol, at least to himself, but sobered up quicker than some of his peers. In 1975, at the age of 21, he grew tired of running from the police and throwing away his youth. He gave up crime for good. It was easier than he thought. Years later, he was on the receiving end when his prized hunting, fishing and work gear was stolen from his car. Dennis lost nearly $20,000 in uninsured power tools in another break-in a few years later. He felt a flood of remorse and sympathy for the people he had hurt in his past. Dennis hated being a victim.

He had suffered through a rough and tumble childhood, growing up in northern Alberta. His dad farmed and hunted and trapped, before dropping dead of a heart attack when Dennis was still a young man. His mother had her hands full raising Dennis, his five brothers and one sister, all by herself, with very little extra money to go around. The boys helped out however they could, hunting and trapping food, just like dad. Mom always carried a heavy heart after losing Dennis's twin brother during birth. Dennis deeply regretted never meeting his twin. His mother died two years after his father, also young, also heart-related. Some people figured it was broken.

Dennis married young, and regretted it almost instantly, separating after only a short time together in the mid 1970s. The relationship did produce a daughter, now 24. He and his ex-wife fought constantly, and weren't meant for each other. Dennis was no angel, often letting his drinking get the best of him. These were not happy times. His first wife even fought him on the divorce he filed for, and the proceedings dragged out for several years. She remarried, to a man with some financial means, and Dennis resisted paying child support as much as he could, partly because he didn't think she needed it, and partly because he couldn't afford it.

Elaine Sand has a warm, caring smile that makes most people who meet her instantly feel good. She's quick to offer guests a cup of coffee from a pot she never allows to get empty throughout the day. It is a staple in this family, dark, with no sugar. Elaine is always up for a conversation, but prides herself on being a good listener, never quick to judge, never one to show much emotion.

Elaine also married young, and divorced quickly. In the late 1970s, Elaine met Dennis, who was dating her then sister-in-law, coming off his crippled marriage. At the time, both Elaine and Dennis were living in the small central Alberta town of Morinville, where Elaine's father was running the local hardware store. Both were coming off bad relationships, and immediately had something in common, finding strength in each other. Within months, Elaine was pregnant with Robert, who was born in December 1978 – just months after Dennis's estranged wife gave birth to their first, and only, child. Dennis paid tribute to his father by naming Robert after him. He and Elaine usually called Robert "junior", as did those closest to him. Less then a year later, Elaine was pregnant again, and Danny was born in June 1980. Months later, number three was on the way. Elaine gave birth to Dusty in June 1981. With three young boys to feed, and their bond growing stronger, Dennis and Elaine finally married in 1986. It was one of the happiest days of both their lives.

Elaine came from an Aboriginal family of little means with some tragedy in their lives. Born in Athabasca, about an hour north of Westlock, Elaine, her three brothers and two sisters were moved to the Northwest Territories as young children. Her mom, an alcoholic, was of little help to her dad, who worked long hours in logging and construction. Elaine's mom was a diabetic, and one day, in the dead of winter, she suffered a seizure while walking home after a night of drinking. She collapsed in the snow and never got back up, her frozen body found the next day. Elaine hadn't hit her teens yet, and her mother was gone.

As a young girl, Elaine had dreamed of a career in law enforcement. At 16, she got a job with the RCMP in Fort Simpson, Northwest Territories. Her official job title was matron, but it felt more like a babysitter, counsellor and peace-maker. Elaine would help strip search female prisoners, usually locals who got carried away drinking, then took a swing or two at their husbands, boyfriends, or maybe both. Elaine loved the responsibility, but was angry at the treatment of some prisoners by police officers. One day, a male friend was arrested for being drunk and disorderly. Although she didn't witness it, Elaine was told after the police had roughed him up and verbally abused him. That was the last straw, and she abruptly quit. Her policing career was finished.

Elaine and Dennis always tried their best for the boys. "Never raise a hand to a lady," Dennis would tell Robert, Danny and Dusty. And they didn't. Dennis advocated working hard, taking responsibility for your actions, and never backing down from anything. He was blue-collar to the core, and he had raised his three boys accordingly. What he lacked in education, he tried to make up in determination and perseverance.

But Dennis didn't always lead by example. His checkered past always seemed to follow him around, and Dennis and his sons were no strangers to random police spot checks as they drove about the community. Dennis always told his boys to respect the law, but sometimes even he had trouble following his own advice.

When the Sand boys were young, still elementary school age, police paid a visit to the family home. Dennis had fallen behind on his payments, and the police were there to arrest him on a court order. A mini-scene ensued, with heated words being exchanged as the boys looked on, crying that their daddy was being taken away. Dennis returned a short time later, but complained openly about the treatment he'd received from the courts, his ex-wife, and the police. Robert never forgot that scene, and would often replay it in his head.

* * * * * *

It didn't take Robert long to gather his few belongings, pack a bag, and walk out the front door of Stan Daniels, leaving only a CD player behind. Laurie was waiting for him on the street outside, as he'd told her to on the phone. She had been so excited, which re-assured Robert he'd made the right choice.

Robert wanted to call his parents, but knew he would upset them. He figured he'd wait a few days, once they got out of the area, and break it to them gently.

Robert, and Danny, had given their parents too many fits to count, beginning in their early teens when they began experimenting with drugs, using most of their allowance to buy a few grams of marijuana. Elaine saw their money vanishing, especially Danny's, and tried to intervene. Although Danny was furious, Elaine dragged him to a drug rehabilitation centre when he was 14, then lived with him in the centre for a full week, hoping he'd come out clean. Danny and Robert wouldn't hide their drug use when confronted by their parents, but would always say "it's what everyone is doing".

Robert and Danny also learned how to make a quick buck the easy way. Their first introduction to this was courtesy of a con artist in the Westlock area, who recruited the still pre-teen boys to steal his truck, then burn it, as part of an insurance fraud scheme. It was the easiest $500 they had ever made.

The boys did work for some of their money, picking rocks and clearing land for neighbours. They were respectful of their older customers, especially women, and could occasionally be seen in town opening the door for a woman, or helping a grandmother load groceries into her trunk. Of course, it was just as likely they had just stolen from the grocery store the grandma was coming from.

Dennis and Elaine were fighting a losing battle. One time, Danny took the family's home movie collection and sold it for drug money. Elaine was livid, and turned Danny in to the police. He was charged with theft, convicted, and given probation. Dennis also turned his boys in after catching them once stealing cars. But the tough love seemed to backfire, with the courts giving them a slap on the wrist, and Danny and Robert becoming more cunning.

Elaine once cut off the boy's allowance, convinced they were throwing all the money away on drugs. Danny and Robert just stepped up their criminal ways, figuring it was easier to steal than work for the money.

While Dusty learned to negotiate his way out of difficult situations, Robert, and especially, Danny would let their emotions rule, often resulting in violence. Danny began throwing his weight around once he hit his early teens, always doing it with a smirk that left his peers and teachers concerned. He was a regular visitor to the principal's office, where he occasionally vandalized the walls or his own body during violent outbursts. In his younger years, teachers tried strapping him, but Danny showed a high tolerance of pain and little remorse. Suspensions didn't work either – both Danny and Robert viewed them more as holiday than punishment.

* * * * * *

A warrant was issued for Robert's arrest on December 11, after he missed his curfew for the second straight night, and all indications were he wasn't coming back. An Alberta judge had also issued a warrant for Laurie when she failed to appear in court the previous day. There was no turning back now. Robert and Laurie were officially on the run.

The two fugitives headed over to Danny's apartment – Robert wanted to speak with his brother in person about their plans, to see him one more time before he and Laurie moved on. They arrived in the evening, and were surprised to find Kevin, Danny's roommate, home as well. Kevin had left work early that day, after being kicked by a cantankerous cow. Danny, who had also been grazed by a hoof, was still laughing about it when they arrived. Kevin didn't find it as funny, but time off was time off.

Robert told Danny he was planning to flee the province, and was going to bring Laurie with him. Danny, who had earlier pleaded with his brother to stay, quickly offered his help. Danny knew he wouldn't change his brother's mind, so he didn't waste any time trying. Danny asked Kevin if he would give them a ride to Red Deer, which was less than an hour south of the city. Danny lied to Kevin, saying his brother had to meet a friend. Kevin reluctantly agreed to give the Sand boys and Laurie a ride.

They arrived in Red Deer under the cover of darkness, and Danny directed his roommate to a fenced-in compound on the outskirts of town. Laurie was asleep in the back, while Robert was thrilled his brother was now willing to help him in his time of need. But that was Danny, always wanting to impress his big brother, to make him proud. And Robert was proud, even if he didn't show it very often. Kevin was uneasy, worried about what was to come, but also felt loyal to Danny, whom he'd come to respect and admire. But he sensed there was a lot more to this then just meeting a friend.

Danny ordered Kevin to stop the car, got out and began climbing a high barbed-wire fence. Robert and a very sleepy Laurie stayed behind with Kevin. Within a few minutes, they all heard the sound of an engine firing up, saw the flash of headlights coming on, and watched as Danny drove a blue GMC pickup truck straight through a gate, out of the compound and on to the street. With a big smile on his face, Danny got out, wished his brother well, and watched Robert and Laurie to get inside with their bags and drive away. Danny the parolee had just broken the law, but this one was easy to justify in his mind. Robert had needed him, and he'd come through. That's what brothers were for. Robert and Laurie sped away, seated side-by-side.

* * * * * *

Edmonton police were quick to react after learning Robert Sand was on the loose. His previous crimes, including the attack on police, were red-flagged on his file, meaning Edmonton's finest would pull out all the stops to find him. In the hours that followed the issuing of his warrant, police visited the homes of Dennis and Elaine and Elisabeth. All of them told police the truth – they didn't know where Robert was. Danny called his parole officer, admitting he'd seen his brother the previous night and knew he was on the run. Danny had wanted to be up front with his parole officer, just to keep the heat off him should Robert need him again. But in a moment of absolute stupidity which he quickly regretted,

Danny asked if the police would be checking his apartment, a question which earned him an immediate visit from Edmonton officers, who found nothing but spent several hours questioning Danny.

Elisabeth wasn't surprised when she returned home with her brother to find police waiting for her. She knew it was about Robert, the police didn't have to tell her that. Elisabeth blamed much of this on Laurie, for stripping away the Robert who had been planning for a family Christmas and a future, and turning him into a fugitive. Once police had left, a frantic Elisabeth called Danny.

"What's going on?" she demanded, expecting he probably knew.

Danny had been waiting for a call from Elisabeth, and it bothered him that she was caught in the middle of this.

"If Rob needs me, I'm going to go," Danny said matter-of-factly.

Elisabeth was frozen with fear. "Are you dumb? Rob has done enough for himself already. Rob can take care of himself," she said.

Danny told his "little sis" it was going to break his heart to be away from his "big bro", that Robert would need someone to watch his back. When Robert and Laurie had driven away the previous night, Robert had promised to call soon with an update about their location, and plans. Danny was now waiting anxiously for that call. Before they hung up the phone, Danny told Elisabeth he loved her, then made one final promise to his favourite girl.

"There's no way I could go back to prison," he said, "I would rather die."

* * * * * *

Robert and Laurie, buoyed by a sense of adventure and excitement, were also plagued by a fear of the unknown. They both knew warrants would be out for their arrest, although the police would probably only be worrying about Robert. It was December 13, and Robert and Laurie had spent the night driving back towards Westlock, but Robert knew he couldn't go home. The cops were probably waiting outside his parents' trailer, and even if they weren't, Dennis and Elaine would likely turn him in the second he walked through the door. They'd done it before, and Robert knew this time would be no different. But Robert did know somebody who had protected him in the past, and old friend he could always count on. As he and Laurie headed north up the highway, Robert made a right turn at the Westlock cut-off, taking him in the opposite direction of his hometown. They were headed to Clyde.

Deep into the dense forest, down a series of poorly maintained, narrow, winding roads, past numerous rugged looking properties filled with "Do Not Trespass" signs, sits the home of Sharon Ford. Robert spent a lot of good years out here, visiting his best friend, Richard Ford, before the young man died tragically right before Robert's eyes. Robert didn't get out here as often these days, where Sharon continued to live a spartan life, but it still felt like home whenever he did. In a time of need, Sharon was always there. Robert wanted to take Laurie to meet the special woman in his life, who never held a grudge and was always quick to overlook one's faults and focus on the positive. But before they arrived, Robert had other business to take care of. They had spent nearly a full day in the same stolen truck, and Robert knew that was too long for one vehicle. The simple solution to a minor problem – just steal another truck. They were easy pickings in these parts, where yards were vast and people-sightings infrequent.

Andrew Weiler, a lanky 28-year-old rancher who stands about six-and-a-half feet tall, is an imposing sight. During the early evening hours of December 13, Weiler was tending to his cattle when he spotted a truck sitting on the road just outside his property. Suspicious, he drove his tractor towards the truck and noticed it was empty. He returned to his field and was headed towards his driveway when a man, wearing a neck warmer pulled over his nose, emerged from behind his truck and walked towards him.

Robert didn't waste any time cutting to the chase.

"I'm gonna steal your truck," he said to the farmer, taking a casual approach and pointing directly at the 1972 Ford pick-up behind him.

"Beat it," Weiler said, undeterred.

Robert was taken aback. At this point, there were two options – beat the shit out of this clown, or try to talk to him. Robert knew which Danny would have chosen if he were there, but Robert elected for the verbal route.

"Look, I'm in some trouble. Somebody is hurt in my truck, which is out of gas. If you don't give me your truck, I'm going to have to take the keys from you," said Robert, who could make up an instant lie with the best of them. Robert also told Weiler he was armed with a gun, which was another fib. Weiler refused to budge, and Robert's patience began to wear thin.

"Just let it go. It's just a fucking truck. It's not worth it," he told the man.

"That's not the idea here. You're taking something that's mine," Weiler responded.

The pair continued their bizarre discussion for about 15 minutes, and Weiler finally agreed to hand over the keys when Robert became more aggressive. Robert got into the truck, shouted at Weiler for not having much gas in it, then drove away, stopping to pick Laurie up from their other vehicle at the end of the driveway. Weiler wasn't quite ready to let go, however. He sprinted to his shed, grabbed his trusty shotgun and took aim at his fleeing pickup. Weiler fired two shots, into the air, hoping to scare the hell out of the thieves. Robert and Laurie, startled by the loud blasts, sped away. Sitting next to them, stuffed down the side of the seat, was a Bible.

* * * * * *

A huge smile washed over Sharon's face as she embraced Robert, while a weary Laurie stood beside them. Robert said Laurie had hit rock-bottom, but he was helping her get back on her feet. After a few hours, Robert dropped a bombshell, telling Sharon they were actually on the run from the law. Sharon was stunned.

"Don't be stupid," she said, in the best motherly voice she could muster. But Robert wouldn't listen, not this time. He couldn't stand the pressure of having so many sets of eyes watching him constantly, waiting for him to make a mistake. No, this time, Robert was going to take charge. He was breaking free of the restraints, and taking Laurie with him.

Laurie wanted to tell her family the good news, especially since she didn't know when she would see them again. It was December 14, and she hadn't touched drugs for a week, thanks to Robert. The couple left Sharon's residence early, heading up the highway towards Athabasca.

Laurie wanted to visit her sister, Andrea Reid, and introduce her to Robert. They arrived in mid-afternoon, and Laurie immediately ran over to her niece, Reyanne, giving the four-year-old a giant hug. Laurie loved children, although she hadn't been around many lately. Laurie helped the girl finish baking and icing cookies. It was close to evening when Laurie told her sister the real reason for her visit.

"Andrea, I'm trying to get off the drugs, to turn my life around," said Laurie. She mentioned wanting to get out of Edmonton, but didn't tell her sister about the criminal charges she was running from. Robert, feeling slightly out of place, sat quietly on a couch while the two women chatted. Laurie went to go have a shower, and get some clean clothes from her sister, while Robert politely asked Andrea for a glass of water. After leaving her sister's home, Laurie and Robert headed towards her mother's home for a brief visit.

Donna Bell hadn't seen her daughter for what seemed an eternity, and while she always worried, she no longer allowed Laurie's lifestyle to control her own life. Donna was happy to see Laurie, who proudly introduced Robert as the man who was helping to clean her up. Donna was sceptical, but supportive of her daughter's efforts. But Donna had a sense of déjà vu, as they had gone down this road to rehabilitation before, only to quickly take a wrong turn and get lost. Laurie mentioned possibly going back to school, before she and Robert said they had to get going for the next stop on their whirlwind tour of town – the Union Hotel.

* * * * * *

Margaret Howse was tending bar on a rather quiet Friday night when Laurie walked in, Robert at her side. Laurie was looking for her father, who hadn't been home when they went knocking at his upstairs suite. Howse hadn't seen Neil Bell that night, but told Laurie she'd tell him she stopped by. Laurie and Robert sat down at a table, along with a few locals who bought them drinks. Neither Robert nor Laurie had much money on them, so the gesture was appreciated. Soon, a few of the people at the table were lighting up some pot.

Howse began to worry about the company Laurie was keeping, knowing the teen was already fragile. Laurie, who had come to Athabasca partly to celebrate a full week of keeping clean, was fighting the urge this night, as those around her smoked up. She walked over to a ragged looking patron, sitting at a table near the end of the bar, and asked him for some speed. The man said he didn't have any. Laurie was getting fidgety, and began pacing back and forth, while Howse walked over to the table where Robert and the locals were sitting. It was now 1 a.m., and she had seen just about enough. The smell of marijuana was wafting over to the bar, and Howse told them all they would have to leave. Slowly, the table got up, including Robert, who joined Laurie and walked out of the bar. As they exited the front doors, they were greeted by the sight of an RCMP officer.

CHAPTER FIVE

Trouble never strayed very far from the Union Hotel, especially on a weekend. Const. David Evans and the rest of his colleagues with the Athabasca Royal Canadian Mounted Police knew this well, and kept close watch on the town's local watering hole. Catching an unruly drunk, or breaking up a heated scrap, was like shooting fish in a barrel. Especially when it was closing time, which wasn't always recognized by some patrons; lost souls whose social calendars were as empty as the bottles at their table.

On this Friday night, Evans was doing his usual patrol through town when he came across a typical scene outside the bar. A man, barely able to stand upright, was drinking beer while standing on the sidewalk. Evans immediately recognized him as a local drunk, banned from the bar because of a violent history. Beside the man stood a young woman, while another man who'd just left the hotel was quickly walking away down the street. Evans approached the drunk, needing no introduction. But he was curious about the young woman beside him, and asked her for some identification.

Laurie's was nervous, almost sick. Her plans with Robert – fleeing the province, getting a fresh start and falling in love – were suddenly in peril.

Robert appeared to have got away. But that only left Laurie feeling more vulnerable and afraid. She tried to remain calm, but knew a warrant had probably been issued after she skipped court. But giving a false name could only add to her problems.

"Laurie Bell," she said, responding immediately to the officer's question.

The town drunk locked up in the back of his cruiser car, Evans was now free to focus on the young woman before him. It was just a hunch, the kind police officers get through experience, but Evans was suspicious. He sensed she might be hiding something.

Evan asked for some photo identification, but Laurie didn't have any. She told the officer she was from Athabasca, but gave him a friend's address in Edmonton, where she had spent some nights before hooking up with Robert. Laurie stood, frozen, when the officer told her to wait a moment while he returned to his car. He was going to run her name on his computer.

Laurie Bell's name wasn't a familiar one to Evans, who was relatively new to the community. She seemed sober, and in control, but he knew appearances could be deceiving. He punched in the name, and within seconds had a file up on the screen. Evans saw a handful of prior arrests, but nothing serious stood out. There were no warrants on the system, and because standing outside a bar next to a drunken fool wasn't a criminal offence, Evans had no reason to hold her. He left his cruiser car and told Laurie the good news: she was free to go.

It didn't make any sense, but Laurie certainly wasn't going to argue. She thanked the officer, wished him a good night, and walked quickly away from the bar, hoping Robert was just around the corner. He was, greeting her with a giant hug, and the pair were on their way. They had dodged a major bullet.

* * * * * *

The night was still young, and Laurie was feeling high on life. Robert was tired, but glad his girlfriend was still at his side. When he had ducked out of the Union Hotel, Robert was terrified Laurie would get taken away. But her situation wasn't as serious as his, and it would have been too risky for him to stick around. As they walked through Athabasca, breathing in the cold night air, Laurie ran into an old acquaintance.

It had been months since Laurie last saw Russell Wand, as she was spending most of her time in Edmonton. Russell was happy to see her, and mentioned he was having a small party back at his apartment. It was late, but Robert and Laurie felt like celebrating.

It turned out to be a party of four – Robert, Laurie, Russell and his roommate, a man Laurie only knew as Delancey. They chatted for a few minutes, before Robert said he was too tired to stay awake and was calling it a night. He went to sleep in another room, but Laurie declined to join him. She was still buzzing, and felt like she needed time, or something, to calm her down. Russell and Delancey said they had just the thing, pulling out a small bowl of marijuana. Temptation quickly got the best of Laurie, who figured a little pot wouldn't do any great harm in the grand scheme of things. She joined in, smoking up with the two men for a few minutes before Russell said he was too tired to continue. No matter. Laurie and Delancey stayed up for another hour or so, each puff of pot calming her nerves a little more. She told Delancey about her plans to turn her life around, with Robert's help, and how a life of crime and drugs was no longer in her plans. When the pot was finished, she fell into a deep sleep.

* * * * * *

The call Danny Sand had been waiting for finally came early on Saturday December 15. It was Robert, asking once again for his help. Danny knew his big brother would come, and didn't hesitate to pledge his allegiance. He knew Robert would do the same for him, and things like parole and work no longer seemed important, or even relevant. There was family to take care of.

Robert told his brother to meet him in Hondo, a small community just north of Westlock where the Sands had spent time as kids, visiting family. Robert told Danny to bring a bag of clothes. Danny got his roommate, Kevin, to do him one more favour and drive him from Edmonton. Kevin was reluctant, especially after the episode days earlier in Red Deer, but Danny seemed desperate.

They arrived in Hondo, and stopped first at Danny's Auntie Linda's, looking for Robert. Moments later, Robert and Laurie pulled up near the home in a pickup truck. Danny jumped out of Kevin's car, thanked his roommate, and said good-bye before climbing into the truck. Robert leaned out the window, telling Kevin to follow him so they could repay him by filling his car up with gas. Kevin wasn't about to turn down an offer that good, and was led into a yard where two large fuel tanks sat. They belonged to his uncle, Alvin Sand, and Robert said he wouldn't mind if they borrowed some. Robert filled his truck, then Kevin's. As they parted ways, Robert thanked Kevin again.

"Have a good life. And don't worry. No one will ever mention your name," said Robert. Kevin drove away, alone, confused and concerned about Robert's cryptic words, and what it meant for his friend, Danny.

In the distance, Robert, Danny and Laurie drove off together, the two brothers re-united and Laurie along for the ride.

* * * * * *

It was getting late, but the Sand brothers had one more task to take care of. As they drove north out of Hondo, they hit the small town of Smith. Robert and Danny, sitting in the front seat, had their eyes open for another vehicle. It had been more than two days since Robert had stolen the truck they were riding in from that crazy farmer, and the boys knew it was time to move on, to keep their trail as cold as possible. It didn't take long to spot another truck sitting on a sprawling farm property, just on the outskirts of town. And this one had an unexpected gift inside – a shiny .22-caliber rifle. The Sand boys were all smiles, amazed at their luck.

After dumping their old vehicle at a landfill site outside town – and setting it on fire, of course – Robert, Danny and Laurie headed back to Sharon Ford's place in Clyde in their new white Dodge pick up.

Sharon was happy to see Robert again, less enthused Laurie was still with him, and stunned that Danny had joined them. Laurie quickly took up residence on Sharon's couch, staring blank-eyed at the television, showing little energy. After a full night's rest, Sharon confronted the boys about what they had done and where they were headed. It was Sunday, December 16.

Dennis and Elaine Sand had been calling her, hoping she'd seen the boys, and begging her to phone them the second she did. Sharon was also concerned, especially about Robert. She had heard about a violent home invasion in the area that week where an elderly farm couple were brutalized in their home and was worried the Sands were likely involved. She told Robert the suspect description matched him perfectly. Robert told Sharon the truth – he wasn't involved. But he also failed to mention the crimes they had committed. Robert felt guilty Sharon was now involved in his mess.

Sharon wasn't so easy on Danny, who was always dragging Robert down into the gutter with him, ever since they were kids. She accused him of sabotaging his brother's rehabilitation. As they stood in her kitchen, Danny made a brash, bold statement that caught Sharon off guard.

"I won't be taken alive," he said.

Sharon's anger only intensified, demanding Danny tell her what he meant. Danny said one of their plans was to go to British Columbia, stealing cars along the way, burning the ones they no longer had use for to get rid of the evidence. In fact, they had already started, Danny said. Sharon's worst fears were confirmed. Danny continued, saying he and Robert would rather die than go back to prison. They had come too far and been through too much to let anyone stop them.

"That way my parents would only have to go to a funeral, rather than visit their sons in jail," he said.

* * * * * *

Elisabeth was frantic. Her numerous calls to Robert's cell phone went unanswered, and he wasn't returning her many messages. And now she couldn't reach Danny. While eating Sunday brunch with her mother at a Westlock restaurant, Elisabeth finally reached Danny on his cell phone. She had been calling him steady since Robert disappeared, begging him to stay out of his brother's mess, and this conversation was no different. But Danny, who could usually talk her ears off, wasn't interested in conversation this morning. He told Elisabeth he had been up all night, and needed to get some sleep. Elisabeth felt like crying, her mind racing at what could have kept Danny up all night.

"Elisabeth, take care of yourself," Danny said in a serious tone.

"I always do," she said.

"Always remember that I love you," said Danny.

"I love you too," she said, and then Danny abruptly hung up.

Sharon decided to approach Robert, making sure Danny was nowhere in sight and Laurie was still asleep on the couch, to tell him about Danny's dire prediction. She pleaded with Robert to go back to Stan Daniels, get away from his brother and go back to focusing on his own life and future. She tearfully reminded him of Richard's death, the affect it had on both of them, and said she didn't want to bury another son. Her tearful plea and the fact she'd called him her son, moved Robert and he said he'd speak to Danny.

Danny denied telling Sharon they had a death wish, and Robert didn't push the issue any further. He chose to believe his brother, and didn't want to argue with Sharon. Instead, he told her they would have to move on soon, that they didn't want to bother her anymore. Sharon knew the real reason, that they were on the run from police, and in a last-ditch effort to protect Robert, gave him some advice. His long, dark hair – the first thing most people noticed about Robert – was going to be his undoing. Sharon suggested he cut and colour it. Laurie sprang from the couch at the suggestion, which Robert reluctantly agreed to. He loved his hair, but cherished his freedom even more. Laurie braided his locks, then cut them, one by one. Sharon had blond hair dye and Robert was transformed before their very eyes, looking more like a surfer than a fugitive. Sharon also told Robert to get out of the province, as quickly as possible.

Elisabeth's worst fears were confirmed that night. Danny's final words from earlier in the day were ringing in her head, and Elisabeth needed to speak with him again. Finally, after ducking out of a Christmas party several times to call, Danny's roommate, Kevin, answered the phone at their Edmonton apartment. Kevin said Danny had left abruptly, taking his things with him. Kevin had driven him to meet Robert and Laurie in Hondo, and hadn't seen or heard from them since. He told Elisabeth what Robert had said, about having a good life. Elisabeth hung up the phone and immediately called Dennis and Elaine, telling them Danny had now joined up with Robert. Christmas was just over a week away, but the Sand family celebration appeared to be on hold.

"The boys are together. They're not coming back," Dennis told his wife.

* * * * * *

A new day, and a new week. Monday, December 17, and it was almost time to say good-bye to Sharon and hello to the unknown which lay ahead. First stop was Rochester, where Robert, Laurie and Danny ditched their current pick-up truck for another. Once again, another prize – inside the 1990 GMC Sierra 4X4 was a .22 caliber rifle, which went nicely with the .22 they'd found two nights earlier. For the fugitives, the best defence was going to be a good offence.

After taking it for a spin in the countryside, the trio stopped at a farmhouse near Clyde, and played trade-in once again. This time, it was a 1990 Chevy Silverado, with Laurie finding a lovely blue winter jacket inside to keep her warm. Robert and Danny drove the hell out of the truck, to the point the motor began smoking and steaming, a problem easily fixed, as the gang completed the stolen car hat trick by ripping off another truck near Rochester.

After spending a passionate night with Laurie, Robert was feeling re-charged. They had guns, they had cars, and most importantly, they had each other. And while his thoughts drifted occasionally to his parents and Elisabeth, Robert was focused on getting out of Alberta and making a clean start with Laurie. He had called his mom, just to say hi, and she had been frantic on the phone, pleading with Robert to turn himself and Danny in. Robert said that couldn't happen.

"If it wasn't for Laurie, you wouldn't be there," Elaine, fighting back tears, told her son.

"Mom, I feel sorry for her. I'm doing this for her," said Robert. He told his mom he loved her, but couldn't promise when he'd be home. Robert also gave Elisabeth a call, knowing she'd be worried. He didn't tell her where they were, but mentioned he missed her. Elisabeth said everyone important to him and Danny wanted them home, safe. Robert said he understood, but it just wasn't possible.

Robert and Danny debated their course, with Danny wanting to go west, and Robert and Laurie east. The loving couple had it all mapped out, perhaps a quaint little home on the ocean, watching sunsets and the tides rolling it. It would be beautiful.

They all agreed they had to go somewhere, that driving around in circles in central Alberta was a recipe for disaster. They also agreed they needed some money, to buy beer, maybe some light drugs, and to crash in a hotel room or two along the way. Robert and Danny had emptied out their bank accounts, which wasn't much. They began heading east, towards the town of Thorhild.

* * * * * *

"Dec. 18, 2001. The last week has been very adventful cuz now I'm awol, and on the lamd." Robert was writing in his diary, while Danny drove and Laurie slept. Spelling was never a strong point for him, but that didn't matter. He continued. *"I talked to my mother and she sounds worried and she would like me to turn myself in and go see a doctor. And as for my dad, well, I not sure how he feels. I just hope he can help mother not worry so much. Well, now I have two travaling partners. My brother Dan who is sometimes worry some. And he's very hard to control when he gets going. And of course I'm with the wonderful Lori. She is so much better now, and so beautiful. We've slept together twice and she is so good. But other than our sex, our bond is pretty quiet. I think cuz she don't let off with much and I let off with less. But her and Dan get along well. They keep each other company."*

* * * * * *

It was early Tuesday afternoon and a steady flow of customers were coming in and out of the Bank of Nova Scotia in Thorhild, about a 40 minute drive east of Westlock. Business was always brisk this time of year, with Christmas shoppers squeezing every cent they could out of their bank accounts. It was as quiet and sleepy a town as they come, where people still left their doors unlocked, parents felt safe even if their kids were out of sight, and everybody knew everybody. But like a summer storm that comes out of nowhere, things were about to change quickly, with Robert, Danny and Laurie approaching town.

Dressed in dark clothes, Robert went over the plan with his brother. Robert would carry the rifle, while Danny would scoop up the cash. Laurie would wait in the truck, and they promised to be in and out within a minute or so. Neither man had robbed a bank before, but they were always game to try something new. And besides, they were desperately low on cash, so this was a necessity. Robert and Danny jumped out of the truck, while Laurie was waiting down the road in yet another vehicle they had stolen. The plan was for the Sands to flee the bank, money in hand, and meet her to switch vehicles, As they approached the front of the bank, Robert and Danny pulled their baseball caps down over their eyes, leaving just enough room to see.

"This is a robbery. Everybody please stay calm!" Robert shouted at the three female tellers and few customers who were inside the branch. He saw a few other people run outside from the vestibule, terrified looks on their faces. Brought up to show respect to senior citizens, Robert allowed two elderly customers to leave.

Danny handed one of the tellers a duffel bag they had been carrying some of their possessions in, which Robert ordered be filled.

"No dye packs, please," said Robert, keeping his voice calm and level, not trying not to alarm the tellers and customers anymore than necessary. He did, however, point the rifle directly at the woman while giving his instructions. The teller, who Robert figured had never seen a bank robbery outside of television or movies, was clearly afraid but did exactly as told, placing several stacks of $20 bills inside the bag. Danny, meanwhile, demanded another teller take him to the vault. The teller said there would be a delay, that it was on a time-locking system. Danny was frustrated, but saw Robert appeared to be cleaning up. He told his brother there was no other money to be had. Robert was worried about the time, knowing an alarm probably had been tripped, so he grabbed the bag and ran, Danny right behind him. They got outside the bank, jumped in the truck and sped towards the meeting point where Laurie was waiting. As they began to drive away, Robert was jolted by a muffled explosion.

Red smoke poured from the duffel bag. Robert opened it to find the bag covered in red paint, some of which sprayed on to the windows of the truck.

"Shit!" Robert screamed, knowing they'd been screwed. Danny was wild with anger, demanding they go back in the bank and kill the teller. Robert knew his brother was crazy and upset enough to do it, but time was their enemy now. They drove away, leaving $4,000 in dye-soaked money behind.

* * * * * *

The robbery couldn't have gone any worse. Their technique inside the bank had been flawless, they thought, the execution perfect. Nobody was hurt, they were out quickly, and they had a bag full of money to boot. But a bank teller had got the best of them, and neither man liked that. At least the escape had gone smoothly, as the Sands had met with Laurie, ditched the robbery truck and driven away in the getaway vehicle without any problems. Robert and Danny vowed things would be different from now on, that they wouldn't be so trusting, or so passive. Laurie's heart was still pounding, and she wished she had something to calm her back down.

The gang drove for about an hour, heading east out of Alberta, before they hit the town of Gibbons. Thinking police would be blanketing the area for the bank robbers, they wanted to keep them guessing by continuing to leave a trail of stolen cars in their wake. This time, they found a quiet farmhouse with a long, extended driveway. Laurie waited in the truck, while Robert and Danny got out to explore. As they walked towards the property entrance, the boys were startled by the sound of an approaching vehicle. Both men remained calm as a woman drove by them, took a quick glance their way, and continued up the driveway to the property. Once she was out of sight, the Sands got into a 2001 Chevy Silverado parked at the end of the driveway. They quickly hot-wired it, then drove over to Laurie and picked her up, leaving their getaway truck behind.

The trio drove down the highway, Laurie sorting through several hundred CDs which were inside the truck. Rob Zombie, Motley Crue, ZZ Top, AC/DC and Shania Twain would keep them company. As they tapped their toes and banged their heads, the group noticed an On-Star tracking device. Robert and Danny made short work of that, ripping the antenna from the truck. They were past the point of no return, and getting caught was not an option.

* * * * * *

In a Westlock grocery store, Elaine ran into Sharon, who casually mentioned that Robert, Laurie and Danny had been by her place in recent days, only to leave abruptly.

"For God's sake, Sharon, why didn't you tell me?" a visibly upset Elaine demanded.

"Because I knew what you would have done. You would have turned them in," said Sharon. Elaine said nothing more, hating Sharon for keeping it from her and, in some ways, hating herself that in their time of need, Robert and Danny had turned to Sharon, and not her.

Elaine had always been close her with three sons, devoting her life to raising them while Dennis was away at work. Their bond was strong, but Elaine felt there had been a great disconnect, especially with Robert and Danny, in recent years. She spent many hours awake at night, thinking about the good times but torturing herself over the bad times, wondering where she and Dennis had gone so wrong.

When the boys were younger, they had always wanted to involve themselves in Elaine's life, often with humorous results. Elaine loved to sing, and was very good, so good that Robert, Danny and Dusty had told her when they were young she should do it professionally. Elaine stopped just short of chasing that dream – she began running her own karaoke business, called "Sunshine Singing DJ Service", in the mid 1980s, before the drunken bar pastime had really taken off in Canada. Elaine focused much of her business on private functions – wedding receptions, office parties, anniversaries – and even brought the boys along to help. It was a great way to get out of the home, meet some new people, and have some fun, while flexing her artistic muscles at the same time. One of Elaine's most cherished possessions is an audio tape of Robert, Danny and Dusty singing to their grandfather, her dad.

"Grandpa...tell me 'bout the good ol' days. Sometimes, I feel like...this world's gone crazy," the sweet-sounding, high-pitched boys belt out, almost in unison, most definitely off-key, but still fabulous. The boys also sang to Dennis, mastering "Daddy's Hands" – a song he held dear to his heart.

Dennis would also search through his past, wondering where he failed his boys. Was it his criminal past, the lingering bitterness with police? Dennis felt he had always tried his hardest, despite never holding down a steady job for long, doing whatever he could to make a buck. He tried his hand at trapping, working on a chicken farm in nearby Thorhild, helping on a dairy farm in Clyde, and taking a run at cattle and grain farming in Westlock. He spent several more years working in the Alberta oil patch, and now made his living working for the County of Westlock.

In the late 1990s, the Sands moved to a tiny, isolated trailer park just outside of Westlock, close to the even smaller community of Pickardville. The trailers are nice enough, with Elaine Sand decorating the outside with a gorgeous rock garden stocked with fish. Inside, teddy bears are everywhere, a love Elaine carried on from childhood. "Home, Sweet Home" is etched on the kitchen cupboards. A black guitar rests against a leather couch, and next to the karaoke machine, showing the family's love of music is never far away. Dennis has hung hunting photographs and antler trophies in the living room. A greenhouse sits in the back, both a hobby and necessity for the Sands. No dinner is complete without some freshly-picked garden vegetables. Just next to the greenhouse is the henhouse, where the family's pet rooster greets all visitors, and provides early-morning wake-up calls to the trailer park. Three hens help the family earn a little extra income – an "eggs for sale" sign sits in front of the home, visible to all driving by on the main road.

The boys were always given a modest allowance, in exchange for helping around the home, but Dennis and Elaine couldn't afford much. They saw some of the other parents who bought their teen's new cars, all-terrain vehicles, fancy bicycles, and knew they couldn't do the same for their kids. Family vacations consisted of trips to the Narrow Lakes campground, about 60 kilometres northeast up the highway. The Sand family loved to camp, and the boys quickly learned about wilderness survival in the rugged Alberta forests. They may not have attended Boy Scouts, but Dennis always believed experience was the best teacher.

The Sand family moved around often with Dennis's varied jobs. The Sand brothers first attended Eleanor Hall elementary school in Clyde. Robert and Danny quickly bonded with two other boys, Richard Ford and Nathan Tippel. They shared a common love for adventure, but felt a unique bond – of all the kids in their class, they were the only ones of mixed race in a white bread town. Nathan, half Chinese, and Richard, half black, became especially close with Robert, who was half native. Danny often tagged along with the trio, although Robert, Nathan and Richard would regularly shun him. The boys would sometimes make fun of Danny because he was overweight and lazy. Robert, Nathan and Richard would pick on Danny, and to a lesser degree Dusty, beating them up in play fights which often got out of hand.

The boys were disciplined at home for bad behaviour, with Dennis always quick to dish out a spanking whenever he felt it was deserved. Elaine always made sure Dennis didn't hit them too hard. Robert, Danny and Dusty would also lose privileges, such as use of the telephone, and would be grounded if things really got out of hand.

With his boys fugitives from the law, Dennis now wished he could get his hands on Robert and Danny. He knew the police were looking for them, and worried what would happen if they reached them first.

* * * * * *

The road out of Gibbons had been a smooth one, and the Chevy Silverado was purring like a cat. Of all the vehicles they had stolen, this was Robert, Danny and Laurie's favourite, and they decided they would hold on to it for a while. On Wednesday, December 19, the rolling plains of Alberta gave way to the flat terrain of Saskatchewan. The group was taking turns sleeping, while Robert and Danny would rotate driving. Still seething over the botched bank robbery, money was still a major concern, as was a possible confrontation with police.

They didn't really know where they were headed, and there weren't a lot of places to hide on the Prairies, especially in winter, and run-ins like the one in Athabasca were bound to happen, especially if they were going all the way to the east coast. They had only eaten up a few hundred of the several thousand kilometres they would have to cover, burning through several trucks in the process. Danny still had his heart set on B.C., but Robert and Laurie had convinced him the other side of Canada was a better choice. There would be less heat on them there, less chance they'd be recognized. As the weak mid-winter sun vanished quickly, turning mid-afternoon into evening, the fugitives entered the tiny town of Nokomis, Saskatchewan.

Dennis Simpson was alone in his country home, expecting his wife to return at any minute. Dennis wasn't going to wait for her, as he had some errands to run in town which would only take a short time. At 4:15 p.m., he piled on his winter boots and jacket, locked his door, and drove away from the house. He never saw the truck waiting right around the corner.

Robert, Danny and Laurie had watched the man leave and figured they might only have a short time before he returned.

Although they were armed, they decided to work fast. Robert and Danny wasted no time forcing their way into the house, and the group split up, rushing past the decorated Christmas tree filled with presents. In the sewing room, of all places, they struck gold. A closet, tucked into the corner, was filled with guns. The group quickly converged on the room, and counted 15 different firearms, likely the collection of an avid hunter. Danny and Robert, knowing quality from crap, quickly picked their favourites. A Mossberg .22. A Churchill .303. A Winchester 30-30. They filled a duffel bag they had brought from the car, grabbing hundreds of rounds of ammunition, which they found hidden in a downstairs office and a suitcase in the laundry room. In a matter of minutes, nine high-powered guns were stuffed inside their bag. In the master bedroom, they found cufflinks, an extensive coin collection, and a jewellery box filled with shiny, expensive-looking pieces. The group grabbed all they could.

On their way out, they passed the Christmas tree. Robert and Danny, still carrying some of the guns they couldn't fit in the bag, dumped them on the ground, just under the tree and beside several wrapped presents. Robert briefly thought of the Christmas he was supposed to be having with his family, but took some comfort in the fact Danny, and especially Laurie, were with him. Robert bent down and picked up a small stuffed animal wearing a scarf and red toque. He was going to give it to Laurie.

Sylvia Simpson returned home at 4:40 p.m., a little later than she expected. She noticed Dennis's truck was gone, and reached for her keys to let herself in. But the woman didn't need keys today. Her door was wide open, her home a mess. There was no sign of the thieves who, in about 15 minutes, had shattered the heart of a woman and broken her trust in society.

"Dennis, there are guns all over the house. You have to come home right away," she shouted at her husband, whom she reached by telephone.

Driving away from Nokomis, Robert, Danny and Laurie began searching through their loot, like kids at Christmas. Laurie was especially interested in the jewellery, which appeared to tell quite a story about the people they had just robbed. A gold ring, engraved "Dennis and Sylvia 25 years", was in the pile. Robert slid it on his hand, holding it up and admiring the look. Two sparkling wedding bands were also inside the bag.

Robert, feeling spontaneous, took one of the gold bands, grabbed Laurie's left hand and placed it on her finger. Laurie, in return, put the other one on Robert's left hand. Robert and Laurie stared into each other's eyes, hugged and kissed. It was official. Using another couple's precious rings, they were engaged.

CHAPTER SIX

Dennis Strongquill spent the day rushing around, trying to get to as many friends as possible. It was December 18, a Tuesday, and this would be the last chance the veteran RCMP constable would have to see them before Christmas. Duty called, and crime didn't take a holiday just because the calendar said December 25th. Dennis had volunteered to work through Christmas, so he could get New Year's off. He only had a few hours to make the rounds in his hometown of Barrows before he had to jump in his car and make the nearly three-hour drive to Waywayseecappo.

Although he couldn't be home for Christmas this year, home was coming to him. His girlfriend, Mandy Delorande, was arriving in Waywayseecappo the following night, along with their now seven-week-old daughter, Korrie. Dennis smiled when he thought of the past seven weeks. He felt like a new man, invigorated and full of life – despite losing a few hours of sleep each night. Mandy was bringing her five other children as well, so it would certainly be a full house. They would be staying in a residence just behind the detachment, provided by the RCMP, where they would enjoy their first full family Christmas together.

"Merry Christmas, Ed!" Dennis said, as he walked up to the front door of his long-time friend, Ed Zastre. The two men went way back, to their days working in the area saw mills together, before Dennis had joined the RCMP at the age of 32. Dennis hadn't forgotten his roots, though, and always remembered the people who were important in his life. Zastre considered Dennis a brother, and cherished the time they'd spend together. On his days off, Dennis would usually come by to visit, usually to sit on the porch and talk, or watch baseball on television. He often brought his guitar, and the men would sing together. Sometimes Dennis and Zastre would head into Winnipeg, a five-hour drive, to see a movie, or go shopping. Zastre had even gone out to Powerview, Manitoba, back in the days when Dennis was stationed at that detachment in the central part of the province.

Dennis had a large package in his hand, which he gave to Zastre on the old wooden porch. Zastre, smiling ear to ear, took the gift from his friend. He opened it, revealing a Christmas card and some new weights. He was thrilled. The men talked about their holiday plans, and Dennis said he was looking forward to the New Year's Eve dance at the local community hall. Zastre said he would be there.

"I'll see you on New Year's, then," Dennis said as he walked away with a wave.

Terry Bulycz saw the purple car motoring around Barrows and knew instantly that Dennis was in town. He was sitting on his porch, sipping a beer, when Dennis walked up.

"Do you want a beer?" asked Bulycz, raising his bottle towards Dennis.

"No, I've been fighting that sucker for 10 years," Dennis said with a chuckle.

Bulycz, of course, knew about Dennis's struggle with the bottle, and was happy he'd declined his offer, made simply to be courteous. He also knew about Dennis's wicked sense of humour. One night, when the two men had been playing hockey in nearby Birch River, Dennis had cracked the whole team up when he rushed to get dressed and get home following the game. Jacket on and equipment bag in hand, Dennis walked right out the door – wearing no pants. Dennis wasn't usually so absent-minded, and most of his friends always figured he set himself up for a laugh, even at his own expense. Dennis was like that, always giving to others.

Bulycz and Dennis had grown up together, and Bulycz was proud of his friend, like most people in the community who wanted to see their own do well. Dennis mentioned he was in a hurry, that he had to go into Waywayseecappo to start his shift, but that he wanted to say hello.

"Looks like you're doing some renovations," Dennis said.

Bulycz invited Dennis in to his home for a minute, to show him an addition he'd just finished. Dennis was impressed, but said he had to get going.

"You have a Merry Christmas," Dennis said on his way out the door. He got into his car, and headed for work.

* * * * * *

They were known to many as Old Bull and Young Bull. Dennis Strongquill and Rob Lasson, separated by 25 years in age but seemingly joined at the hip in body and mind. Rob met Dennis a few years earlier while they were at a Rolling Stones concert in Winnipeg. Rob was serving as an auxiliary community police constable in Amaranth at the time, and Dennis quickly took him under his wing, encouraging him to pursue police work. Dennis was there when Rob graduated from the RCMP training academy in 1999. Now the men were working together in close proximity – Dennis in Waywayseecappo, and Rob in nearby Rossburn.

The men laughed whenever they talked about the incident earlier in the year, when Rob got into a fistfight with a local drunk on the streets of Rossburn. Rob was working alone, and found himself quickly overmatched. He grabbed his radio, calling for anyone in the area to help. Dennis was off-duty, but happened to be in the Waywayseecappo detachment just up the highway, picking up some things.

"I'll be right there, buddy!" answered Dennis. The familiar voice brought a smile to Rob's face, and sure enough, Dennis was on scene within minutes. His bright purple Neon was impossible to miss. The drunk took off running into a nearby clothing store, with Dennis and Rob in hot pursuit. They arrested him, only to be confronted by another drunk who claimed to be the man's lawyer.

"All right then, Mr. Lawyer. You're under arrest, too," said Dennis.

Dennis had a magical way with even the most down and out in society. He knew when to crack the whip, but had the softest touch of any cop Rob knew. Dennis would regularly engage those he arrested in conversation, and had a special place in his heart for people battling alcohol addictions. He understood what they were going through. Rob admired those qualities in his good friend.

"You gotta be real careful, Rob," Dennis would often warn.

"You're a similar cop to me. You'll always give people a chance first. But there are people out there who will kill you."

Dennis brought up Rob Thomas, a slain Mountie, when he picked Rob up the evening of December 19 for a quick shopping trip and dinner in Brandon. Dennis had arrived in Waywayseecappo earlier in the day, wanting to get the house ready for Mandy and the kids, who were coming out the next day when he started his shift. The Christmas decorations were hung, the rooms were tidy, but Dennis felt something was still missing – more presents. That's where Rob came in. He was off-duty, and being a bachelor, didn't have any firm plans preventing him from an impromptu road trip. On the drive out, Dennis began speaking of Rob Thomas.

"I can't believe those fucking guys could do that to someone," he said, an unusual amount of anger and emotion in his voice. "That was just such a cowardly act."

They arrived in Brandon and went straight to the Shopper's Mall, where Dennis had a short list of items – picture frames, some clothes, and sexy underwear for Mandy. Rob hadn't planned on buying much – until Dennis found a blue turtleneck sweater hanging on a rack in Sportcheck. The price tag was $95.

"I can't afford that," Rob said.

"All the girls will love it on you," Dennis insisted. Conversations with Dennis always seemed to come back to women, a subject he knew quite well. Dennis loved to flirt, no matter where they were. One time, the two men were doing a walk through the Rossburn Hotel when a female patron stopped to say hello. Dennis grabbed the woman's hand and gave it a gentle kiss.

"Rob did tell me there were a lot of beautiful women in here," Dennis said, as the woman turned to butter. As they walked, Dennis turned to Rob and winked.

"I still got 'er, buddy. But I'm taken now," he said.

As Rob mulled over the purchase of the sweater, Dennis grabbed him firmly by the shoulders, the way a parent takes his child when they have something important to say.

"Buy it, Rob. You only live once. It's only money." Rob bought the sweater.

They went for dinner at Kelsey's that night, where Dennis continued to dole out the advice and wax poetic about their lives.

"You're too young to get married," Dennis told Rob, while adding his own life was the happiest it had been in many years. His health was good, he loved Mandy, and Korrie had given him a newfound sense of being.

The waiter came to take their drink order.

Rob ordered a rum and diet Coke, while Dennis stuck to diet Coke.

"You know what, Rob? They tell me at AA I could probably have a social drink with a friend now, that I could handle that," said Dennis.

"So I'll make you a promise. You and I are gonna have a drink on New Year's Eve."

* * * * * *

A feeling of euphoria was building inside Robert Sand. This town he was in, the name of the motel, even what day it was, didn't seem important anymore. Everyone that mattered right now was in this tiny room, still asleep, maybe dreaming of the life they were soon going to have. And he felt safe, despite knowing he was a hunted man. He had his brother at his side, a truck full of guns, years of life experience and an amazing woman he had quickly fallen in love with, and now planned to marry. It may only have been a few weeks since Laurie came back into his life, but it seemed much longer. He looked at the ring on his finger, smiled, and thought of their future together as husband and wife.

Just last night, they all had a good laugh when Robert checked into the Imperial 400 Hotel in Yorkton under the name "Bob Sandz". As an alias, it wasn't much of a stretch, but it was the best he could do off the top of his head, and it was almost cheeky in its simplicity. Fortunately, the woman at the front counter didn't blink an eye. Nor did she take a second glance at the stolen pickup sitting in the parking lot, waiting to take them on their next adventure. Robert was glad he could make Laurie laugh, and feel safe. He also loved the smile she would flash whenever he called her "my girl".

With Laurie lying next to him in bed, Robert grabbed the stack of papers he had started keeping as a diary and began to write again. It was quiet, a good time to think. His head was clear after a good night's sleep. Robert scribbled quickly, wanting to get his thoughts down as fast as they were racing through his head. Spelling didn't matter. His feelings did.

December 20. I woke up in a motel with a beautiful women beside me. And a rifle and sawed off shot gun close. And I felt really good. Which is better than two days ago when we robbed a bank and went outside to only have a dye pack go off, which made me mad. Cuz I was so nice to the women. And to repay me she throw a dye pack in with my money.

Robert still couldn't get over what that teller had done. They had warned her not to do it, but she didn't listen. She's lucky Danny didn't put a bullet in her, thought Robert. He looked around the room, at the pile of weapons they stole from the farmer, and smiled. Next time, their victims wouldn't be so lucky.

So now I've decided on a new aproch. And it won't be the same or even very nice. Now we've got so much firepower that if a cop pulls us over, he'll be one sorry motherfucker. And I feel so out of control, cuz I've set very few rules. So we can do what ever one wanted. I've got my two favourite people now with me. Dan is great company, but hard to control which agerveats me. And then there's Lori who is now my new girl. And at times I still have no idea who she is. But at the same time I'd love to spend my last days with.

We've got so much more land to cover. And who can tell were our path will lead. I seen a crossroads that looked just like the one I use in my mind when I have to choose a path. And I stopped to have a really good look. And I realized that that's where I was...at a crossroad.

* * * * * *

Robert had always been a leader, in the community, at the playground, in school hallways. Most kids looked up to him, others feared him. Danny was more the follower, but as teenagers, each carved out a reputation as a local legend with the stories seeming to get bigger and better with time. Most people knew the names, and exploits, of Robert and Danny, regardless of whether they'd ever met the boys.

At Eleanor Hall school, the Sand boys quickly established a reputation as troublemakers with little respect for authority. Many teachers quickly wrote them off, especially Danny, who was held back a year at the end of grade two. As a result, he joined his little brother's class the following year. Robert and Danny were seen by their peers as kings of the school, but Robert was clearly in charge. And while the kids admired them, most of the parents looked down on them, not wanting the Sand boys anywhere near their families. They were seen as big-time trouble.

The one person the boys would usually listen to was Dennis. Robert and Danny spoke highly of their father, and always seemed to be aiming to please him. To them, he was almost a larger-than-life hero. Danny often brought pictures of his dad to school, where he would ask teachers if he could use the photocopy machine to blow them up extra-big and take home. He would also bring in pictures of animals the boys and Dennis had trapped – although many teachers believed the prey was caught illegally.

Robert, Danny and Dusty demonstrated a wealth of knowledge about guns. In grade four, Robert and a friend did a school project on ballistics, managing to impress and concern their teacher at the same time. Guns were always present in the Sand household, although Dennis was strict about ensuring his boys weren't reckless. He taught them to hunt deer, moose and elk at a young age, but regularly reminded his sons "never shoot something you wouldn't eat. Guns are not to be played with".

The boys always came to school spotless, scrubbed to the bone, and with lunches that often had the teachers envious. Their mother, Elaine, packed their bags with wholesome goodies such as homemade bread, pies and cakes. Most teachers gave up on the boys when they failed to respond to instructions, or show any initiative. Only a few teachers seemed to get through, asking them, rather then demanding. But no matter what they did wrong, the Sands always seemed to have an answer for everything.

Norma Stasiuk taught music to Robert in grade two, all classes in grade four, and taught Danny and Dusty in grade four. She saw loads of potential in the boys, and was one of few who seemed to register with them. One day, Robert, Danny and a few of their friends shocked Stasiuk when they skipped their lunch hour to begin building a massive haunted house inside her classroom. Following class, they stayed late to continue their work. They arrived early the next morning, and devoted every last minute of free time to the project. Within a week or so, their masterpiece was complete, and the whole school enjoyed the result.

When Danny was in grade four, and Robert in grade six, Stasiuk walked outside on a lunch break to find the pair smoking cigarettes, along with their friends. She didn't rant and rave, like the other teachers would have.

"I see where some of you boys are going to have to be mighty rich when you grow up. You've started a pretty expensive habit," she told them. Stasiuk then called Dennis and Elaine, who were frustrated, but not surprised.

The boys eventually moved on to RF Staples School, where they lived up to their advance billing as bad seeds. Danny, 14, was enrolled in a life skills class, while Robert, 15, began grade 10. Both weren't particularly interested in following the rules at school. Dennis and Elaine would encourage their boys to stick with it, praising them for the occasional good test result or mark. Dennis's shortcomings were exposed in his limited ability to help the boys with their homework, as he was a high school dropout himself. Like father, like sons.

* * * * * *

It was sometime in the afternoon before Laurie and Danny were up, and Robert was struggling with a new plan. While sharing a brunch of beer and marijuana, Robert decided they had left too much damage in their wake to turn back west. The police would surely be looking for them now, and it was too dangerous. Continuing east was the only way.

It was 6 p.m, and time to move on. They were nearly out of pot and beer. Robert, Danny and Laurie lit their last joint and passed it around, taking long drags. Robert had paid for two nights, but they were rested enough to keep going to the next town, wherever that may be. They still had a long way to go to reach the east coast. They would have to watch their money more carefully. Robert left the room key inside the suite, while Danny and Laurie helped gather up and carry the bags of weapons. Laurie made sure to get her bag, with the Christmas teddy bear and movies Robert had given her after they left the farmhouse.

The truck was bitterly cold, having sat all night and day on the frozen Prairie. A light dusting of snow covered the windshield, an early warning of the storm which would blanket the area later that night. Robert jumped in the driver's seat, while Danny sat beside him and Laurie climbed into the back, with the guns safely tucked beside her. Nobody was sure where the road would take them, but it didn't matter. They had each other, and they were happy. Up ahead, Robert saw a sign which read "Welcome to Manitoba".

* * * * * *

Stacy Panasiuk pulled into the parking lot of the Roblin Motor Inn, a few minutes early to pick her friend Lindsay Andres up from work. Andres was waitressing inside the motel restaurant, a crummy job but one which would help pay some Christmas bills and save for university. It was 9 p.m., and Panasiuk was waiting patiently inside her running car, comforted by the heat, as Andres emerged from the motel and walked to the car. The two young women were excited about what the night might offer.

Panasiuk began pulling out of the parking lot when she saw a truck on the highway which made her heart skip a beat. It was her ex-boyfriend. Panasiuk still had some of his clothes in the car, and planned on returning them the next time they ran into each other. It would be less awkward that way, she figured. He was just up the road, and the two women thought now was as good a time as any to give them back. The truck was pulling away, quickly, so Panasiuk flashed her high beams to get her ex-boyfriend's attention. He continued driving, apparently oblivious to her signals. Panasiuk decided she wouldn't chase him down, not wanting to stray too far from Roblin because she had another girlfriend she wanted to visit in town that night. Panasiuk would just drop the clothes off at his house later.

Panasiuk turned her car around, back towards Roblin. In her rear view mirror, she saw the truck pull a sharp u-turn, then drive up behind her. Her ex-boyfriend must have noticed after all. As the truck caught up to her car, a hand appeared through the truck's side window, waving her for her to stop. Panasiuk obliged.

Panasiuk and Andres walked over to the truck, but were shocked to see it wasn't her boyfriend at all. Three strangers were inside, a young woman and two men – one with several tattoos splashed across his bare arms. They were looking for a good time and wanted some advice from locals. One by one, the passengers introduced themselves – Robert Sand, Laurie Bell and Danny Sand, the tattooed one.

Danny asked about the best place to score some weed and whether there were any hot parties that night. He told the young women he was pissed off, having gone to the Roblin Motor Inn earlier wanting a drink, only to get carded. They left, rather than return to the truck to get their ID, and were now looking for another way to pass the night.

Robert felt the stiff winter air against his face as he stuck his head out the window of the moving Silverado. Danny wasn't slowing down, either, and the cold temporarily took Robert's breath away. He wedged half his body out the window, while Laurie screamed with delight, and possibly fear, that the man she loved might just fall right out of the truck at any moment. Robert yelled at the top of his lungs, feeling free and young and crazy. This was their night, their world. Nobody could stop them.

Tire tracks in the snow reveal the final route taken by Dennis Strongquill and his killers, from Main Street into the parking lot of the Russell RCMP detachment where he was ambushed on December 21, 2001. *(Photo courtesy RCMP)*

A close-up view of the passenger side window of a police SUV which was blown out by four shotgun blasts during the fatal shooting of Dennis Strongquill. *(Photo courtesy RCMP)*

The charred remains of the Chevy Silverado which Robert and Danny Sand and Laurie Bell were driving at the time Dennis Strongquill was killed. Police identification markings show where several bullets fired by Strongquill's partner, Brian Auger, struck the truck. *(Photo courtesy RCMP)*

Danny Sand lay dead on the rooftop of the Wolseley Motel in Saskatchewan, a high-powered rifle just beneath his feet. Sand was killed by a police sniper during a standoff just hours after Dennis Strongquill was murdered on December 21, 2001. *(Photo courtesy RCMP)*

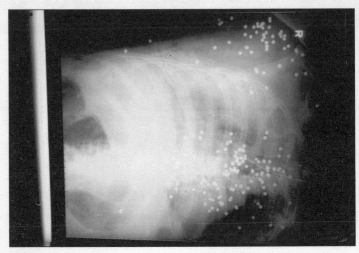

An x-ray of Dennis Strongquill's chest taken during his autopsy reveals dozens of shotgun pellets which pierced his body and killed him. *(Photo courtesy RCMP)*

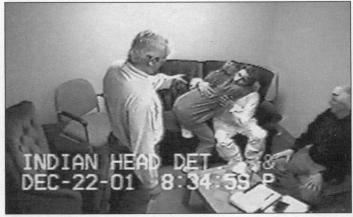

Laurie Bell embraces Robert Sand in the police interview room in Indian Head, Saskatchewan. Investigators Jim Atras and Joe Nowell allowed the young lovers to spend 30 minutes together, provided the video camera kept rolling and they remained in the room. Following the reunion, Sand made good on his promise to give police a full confession. *(Photo courtesy RCMP)*

A police mugshot of Robert Sand taken just hours after his arrest on December 21, 2001 at the Indian Head, Saskatchewan RCMP detachment. (Inset) A previous photo of Robert Sand shows how he had altered his appearance while on the run from police across the Prairies.
(Photo courtesy RCMP)

A police mugshot of a smiling Laurie Bell, taken just hours after her arrest on December 21, 2001 at the Indian Head, Saskatchewan RCMP detachment. Bell claimed the police photographer had cracked a joke about a Garfield tattoo on her buttocks, causing her to laugh just as he snapped the picture.
(Photo courtesy RCMP)

Brian Auger, the partner of Dennis Strongquill, holds Dennis's Stetson and gathers his thoughts while at Strongquill's funeral in late December 2001.
(Photo courtesy Winnipeg Free Press)

Crown and defence lawyers gather in Brandon, Manitoba for the start of Robert Sand and Laurie Bell's first-degree murder trial in April 2003. From left to right – Jim Ross, Bob Morrison, Tammy Baryluk, Brian Midwinter, Jason Miller, Greg Brodsky. *(Sketch courtesy of Dale Cummings, Winnipeg Free Press)*

Laurie Bell and Robert Sand sit side-by-side in their prisoner's boxes in Brandon courthouse, where they were able to regularly communicate with each other during courtroom recesses.
(Sketch courtesy of Dale Cummings, Winnipeg Free Press)

Greg Brodsky, one of the country's most prolific criminal defence lawyers, stops outside the Brandon courthouse to speak with reporters about his client, Robert Sand, and the ongoing murder trial in April 2003.
(Photo courtesy Brandon Sun)

Rose Ferguson, a jailhouse informant who once shared a cell with Laurie Bell, leaves the Brandon courthouse after testifying for the Crown in May 2003. *(Photo courtesy Brandon Sun)*

Sylvia and Dennis Simpson leave the Brandon courthouse after testifying in May 2003. The Nokomis, Saskatchewan couple were the victims of a December 2001 burglary where Robert and Danny Sand and Laurie Bell stocked up on weapons which were used to kill Dennis Strongquill. *(Photo courtesy Brandon Sun)*

CHAPTER SEVEN

A pot roast, with all the trimmings. Mandy, an excellent cook, had done it again. She only arrived in Waywayseecappo at 4:30 p.m on Thursday, December 20, just in time to see Dennis off to work. She also put their newborn daughter, Korrie, down for a late-afternoon nap. It was never easy, leaving Barrows behind and settling in their temporary home on the reserve. But it was worth it, because Mandy and the kids at least got to see Dennis more than once in a week. And with Christmas only five days away, this was no time to be apart.

Dennis had left at 6 p.m. to start his eight-hour shift, the aroma of searing meat and scrumptious potatoes begging him to stay. He had promised to make it back for dinner by 7:30 p.m., and true to his word, showed up on time. You could call Dennis anything you wanted – just don't call him late for dinner.

After gorging on the meal, Dennis rushed out, but told Mandy he would try to sneak back later for another quick visit. Dennis loved family time, and would jump at any chance he had to see his loved ones. He re-joined his partner, Brian Auger, who had also taken a break. The two men knew each other well, having travelled much the same circles during their 20-plus years with the RCMP in Manitoba. Talk quickly turned to their Christmas plans, their families, and, of course, little

Korrie as they cruised the highways and side roads of Waywayseecappo.

Dennis couldn't go more than a few minutes without mentioning his daughter. Just weeks earlier, he drove the entire detachment crazy with his constant updates from Swan River, then Yorkton, where Mandy finally had the baby after several days of false labour. As the evening progressed, Dennis mentioned he would like to go check in on Korrie, and Mandy, when he got a chance. At 10 p.m., with no calls for service waiting, he got his opportunity.

All of the kids, including Korrie, were fast asleep when Dennis walked in. Mandy was thrilled to see him again, and Dennis said he could stay about half an hour, provided there weren't any emergencies.

"It's real slow," he said.

"Just enough time for a crib game," said Mandy, who pulled out the board and cards.

She and Dennis had the same competitive spirit, and never wasted an opportunity to try and beat the other in some kind of game. Cards was their favourite, and Dennis usually took it to Mandy. He chalked it up to raw talent. She chalked it up to dumb luck.

This night would prove no different. Dennis won, quickly, and decisively.

"I skunked you," he said, teasing and taunting Mandy. "You smell!"

Mandy just smiled, happy to have the time with Dennis, even if it meant being compared to a stinky animal.

His time almost up, Dennis walked into the spare bedroom, where Korrie was asleep in her crib.

"Don't wake her up," Mandy whispered.

"I won't," said Dennis with a mischievous smile.

She knew what he was going to do, and sure enough, he did. Dennis tip-toed right into the room, bent down, and rubbed his moustache on Korrie's face. Like she always did, the little girl squirmed and swatted at her suddenly itchy face, but didn't wake up. Dennis, looking like the cat who ate the canary, crept back out the room.

Mandy followed Dennis outside as he was about to leave. He had four more hours left on his shift, and they would certainly be long if it remained as slow as the first few. Dennis, who often had trouble falling asleep when he came home from working the late shift, suggested Mandy go to bed right away, so maybe she could get up when he got home, keep him company. Mandy said she would. As she took a drag on a cigarette, Dennis turned to say good-bye.

"Do you know how much I love you, how much you mean to me?" he asked.

The pair hugged, and kissed, and Mandy watched as Dennis headed back into the night.

* * * * * *

Stacy Panasiuk and Lindsay Andres arrived at the Assesippi Inn in Russell about 11:30 p.m., and went straight to their friend, Curtis Gamey. He was bartending at the often raucous nightspot and would know how to handle those Alberta strangers if they caused any trouble, the girls thought.

Panasiuk told Gamey they had been followed down the highway by two men and a woman, who identified themselves as Robert, Danny and Laurie. The man named Robert had even dangled himself out the window of their speeding vehicle, and Panasiuk worried that wild act was only the beginning.

As he spoke with Panasiuk, Gamey looked down at his closed-circuit television monitor and saw three people walk in. He knew most everyone in this bar, but didn't recognize these three, who Panasiuk and Andres identified as the Alberta strangers. The women couldn't believe they had followed them, first from Roblin, then from Inglis, and now into Russell. They were creeped out, and Panasiuk and Andres decided to leave the bar, rather than risk another meeting.

Robert, Danny and Laurie approached the bar, asking for a shot of rye. Waitress Shannon Johnston took one look at the strangers and asked for identification. They seemed to be of age, but Johnston wasn't going to take any chances, especially around Christmas when liquor inspectors really cracked down.

Danny couldn't believe he was being carded, again, and told the pretty young waitress he would show her proof he was of age. He lifted up his shirt to reveal his tattoos.

Johnston's eyes immediately went to the word "senseless" scrawled on the man's body, not the kind of thing you usually saw in these parts. She noticed several other markings on his arm and chest. Still, she insisted the man and his friends show her some identification, but served them each a shot of rye. Danny, Robert and Laurie quickly slurped it down, then reached for their wallets. Johnston explained the identification was necessary because the inspectors, or even police, would probably be dropping in.

"Look at me, do I look like I like cops? If I saw them, I'd just run. I'd be outta here so fast," Danny told the waitress with a laugh.

Laurie told Johnston they had come from Edmonton and were on a road trip. She said they were going to Saskatchewan, then Vancouver – the shot of liquor clearly going straight to her head and ruining her sense of direction.

Johnston was puzzled, knowing the shortest way to Vancouver from Edmonton was not passing through Saskatchewan and Manitoba first. She figured the poor girl was mixed up, as she seemed tired, and probably had just spent too much time on the road.

Laurie walked over to the bar, and said hello to Gamey. She saw he was wearing a bright orange shirt with the words "Fugitive – You Never Saw Me" scrawled in large letters across the front. Laurie asked Gamey if he wanted to trade shirts. He declined, laughing that he wouldn't be caught dead in a woman's shirt! Laurie said the fugitive logo was quite funny, as she and her two friends were on the run from Alberta. Laurie borrowed a cigarette, and told Gamey they could be in trouble. She asked about travelling the back roads of Manitoba to avoid detection from police. Her lips were getting looser by the minute.

Nicholas Murphy was having a friendly, informal chat with the cute Alberta stranger when her boyfriend shot him a crazed look that quickly wiped the smile off his face. Robert's steely stare seemed to communicate a mix of jealousy and anger. The relaxed atmosphere inside the room was gone, the air now thick with tension.

Now this was more like it. Robert could see the look in the young man's eyes, and loved it. He was in control, his favourite position in the world. Robert took it a step further, telling the man and his friends he had some knives in his truck. He invited them to come outside to see them, but they quickly said no.

Robert and Danny walked over to the slot machines, plugging in a handful of quarters, surveying the room and feeling quite bored by the scene. Robert wanted some more action, so he walked over to a group of men playing pool.

Laurie joined him moments later, and grabbed a cue, asking the other players if she could take a shot. Laurie bent over the table, providing Robert the perfect opportunity to engage in a little playful mischief.

"Do you want a piece of this?" he said to the men around the pool table, as his hand connected perfectly with Laurie's ass.

The clock on the wall said 12:20 a.m. when Robert, Danny and Laurie decided they'd had enough of this place. It was time to hit the road again, with no particular destination in mind. They would keep driving until they were too tired to continue, the cover of darkness offering them the best protection from police. Danny got behind the wheel, while Robert took his regular spot beside him. In the back, Laurie got as comfortable as she could with several bags full of stolen goods and guns in her way.

* * * * * *

David Marohn couldn't wait to get home for the holidays. He had been driving most of the day, and night, after finishing work on the pipeline in Fort McMurray, Alberta. His family was waiting at their home near Riding Mountain National Park. It was late, nearly 12:30 a.m., and Marohn was glad his day was nearly over.

Up ahead, his weary eyes opened wide at the sight of flashing police lights. Marohn checked his speed, which was fine, and figured he must just be running into a Christmas Checkstop program. No worries, as he hadn't been drinking. He kept driving, noticing a truck pulled over by the police. Marohn relaxed, knowing there was nothing stopping him from getting home. The people in the truck, it appeared, hadn't been as lucky.

* * * * * *

Robert, Danny and Laurie had taken a series of turns after leaving the bar in Russell, and they were now on a dark, country road. Traction was poor because of the snow and ice, and Danny was anxious to get back to the highway, before they got completely lost in this foreign province. A thick ice fog hung over the area, and Danny had cranked the high beams for better visibility.

He had passed a sign which said Highway 45 was up ahead. Figuring nobody was around, and not wanting to test his brakes on the slippery road, Danny went straight through the stop sign and turned on the highway. Suddenly, the bright flash of police lights appeared behind him.

Panic filled the truck. Danny was nearly delirious.

"Cops!" he shouted to Robert. Danny was looking to his big brother for advice. Surely Robert would know what to do, how to get them out of this and make everything okay. Their freedom, their lives, were being threatened for the first time since leaving Alberta. Danny had vowed never to go back to prison, but talk was cheap. He was seconds away from eating his words.

Robert, sitting in the passenger seat, remained composed. He knew this would happen, sometime, somewhere, and the fact it was *this* night, on *this* highway, was of little concern. He had played this scene out countless times in his head – a confrontation with police – more so in the last few days when he knew they had been taking greater risks while on the run. But it went back even further than that. In his mind, Robert saw the confrontations police had with his father, the time they let a dog attack one of his friends while she was handcuffed, the time they blamed him for the death of his best friend. No, this time things would be different. Robert would not roll over, letting those pigs, those demigods, tell him what to do, control of his life. Robert would show them they were wrong. Dead wrong. Just like he'd written in his diary – *One sorry motherfucker.*

"Stay calm. Just pull over," Robert told Danny.

Danny couldn't believe it. Was his brother crazy? The cops would surely run their licence plate and see the truck was stolen. And there were probably a million warrants on them by this point.

"Just listen to me. I know what I'm doing," said Robert.

Danny pulled the truck to a stop, just as another vehicle approached in the distance. Robert reached in the back and grabbed one of the already loaded shotguns, a Remington pump action they had sawed down after stealing it from the farm in Saskatchewan, giving it the ability to spray shot in all directions. Robert, clutching the weapon, opened the passenger door, while Danny and Laurie remained inside, not sure what was about to happen.

Robert took a few steps, getting within about six metres of the police SUV. He couldn't see much, thanks to the glare of the car's headlights and emergency lights. There was no sign anyone had come out of the vehicle, but that didn't matter. Robert took several steps in the snow, his feet crunching beneath him. His breathing became sharper, his heart pumping faster. Robert could see the passenger door of the police car begin to open. Robert raised the shotgun to waist level, took a deep breath, and squeezed the trigger.

A tremendous blast pierced the air, and Robert was jolted by the force of the shot. The first lead pellets zinged off the side of the passenger door, just as an officer was opening it. Holding the shotgun steady, Robert fired again, this time directly at the front windshield. The sound of breaking glass filled his ears. He fired twice more, in the same spot, with the same result.

Robert emptied the chamber, and braced for return fire. But none came. Instead, the police Explorer spun its wheels, and began rapidly backing up on the shoulder of the highway. Robert hurried back to the truck.

"Follow it!," an out-of-breath Robert yelled to his brother. "Go, go, go!"

Danny stepped on the gas and began driving towards the police car, which had turned around and was heading back towards Russell. Robert was angry that the cowards were running. The chase was on.

* * * * * *

Rod Mushmanski was having trouble unwinding and figured a final cigarette before bed would help calm his nerves. He left his house nestled on the side of Highway 45, and walked outside to his workshop, where he could puff away in peace. Mushmanski turned on the light, sat down in a chair and began to smoke, keeping an eye on the sky and the snowstorm which was brewing. Staring directly at the highway, Mushmanski could hear the sound of a vehicle in the distance. The sound was growing louder, and he was surprised at how quickly it seemed to be approaching. Suddenly, in a rush of wind there was the quick blur of a vehicle going by the large spruce tree and hedge in his yard. Seconds later, another vehicle flew by. Mushmanski had seen a lot of cars drive by during 30 years of living along the highway, but couldn't believe the speed he'd just witnessed, especially with the bad weather that was moving in. He took a few more drags of his cigarette, turned the light off in the workshop, and returned inside.

Danny was closing in on the police car as the highway darkness began to give way to lights approaching in the distance. The speedometer was flirting with 130 km-h, but Danny still felt in control of the truck. Robert was hanging out the side of the window, as he had done earlier in the night – only this time he had a loaded shotgun in his hands. He took dead aim at the car in front of him.

Robert thought his first shot had struck the back windshield but couldn't be sure. He shouted at his brother to stay on their tail, then fired three more shots in the direction of the fleeing SUV. Glass was raining down on the front of the police vehicle as parts of the back windshield were obliterated by the gunfire. This wasn't quite the way Robert had played things out in his head, where a confrontation with police would be a one-stop, perhaps one-shot, deal. But this was more exciting, and he was revelling in the moment. To Robert, the police were showing their true stripes.

The trucks were now re-entering Russell, and passed a Subway restaurant on the right hand side. The streets were bare of traffic. The police were trying desperately to get away, speeding, swerving, but Danny was doing a great job of staying right behind them. Robert had emptied his second gun, and reached back for a third, this time a high-powered rifle. The weapons haul in Saskatchewan was proving its worth tonight.

The chase turned on to Main Street, tires screeching as they passed Donna's Family Restaurant. There was a police station on the right hand side, and the cruiser appeared headed straight for it.

The police officers went right past a long entrance leading in to the Russell RCMP detachment, but made a sharp, sudden turn into a snowy ditch just past it, narrowly missing a posted speed limit sign of 50 km-h. Danny followed through the ditch.

They only drove a few seconds when the police cruiser began to slow down, unable to go any further because of a line of trees in its way. The Explorer slid sideways, coming to a stop.

This is it, Robert thought.

Danny continued driving through the snow, taking a direct line into the passenger side of the police SUV. Robert gripped the shotgun tightly as Danny smashed straight into the side. Robert, never doubting for a moment what he was about to do, didn't waste any time from his position inside the stolen truck.

Raising the gun, he pointed at the passenger window of the cruiser and began firing. He was only a few metres away, close enough to see that the RCMP logo on the car was riddled with pellets. He fired four shots in all. *Boom, boom, boom, boom.* The noise was almost deafening, the muzzle flash nearly blinding.

Suddenly, a police officer approached on the driver's side, where Danny was sitting. Robert saw the man had a pistol, then heard the crack of gunfire. Bullets were whizzing through the interior of the truck, and Robert could hear Laurie and Danny screaming. Danny shouted he'd been hit, and struggled to control the truck as he tried to throw it in reverse and back up. Glass was flying everywhere, and finally the truck began moving. They hit the highway, leaving the police car behind.

CHAPTER EIGHT

Covered in snow, and sweat, a breathless Brian Auger grabbed Dennis Strongquill's limp hand and felt for a pulse. There was none. He shook Dennis, calling out to him, trying to wake him. Nothing.

Brian was trembling, having just unloaded his pistol into the truck that had ambushed them, only to watch it slither out of sight. He assumed he hit someone inside, but couldn't worry about that now. His entire focus was on his partner. He and Dennis had just been talking about coffee, Christmas, and kids. This whole scene was too surreal, too sickening, to believe.

Dennis hadn't fired a single shot, his gun completely falling apart while trying desperately to fend off the ambush. A left-handed shot, the RCMP had given Dennis a right-handed gun, which caused a release mechanism for his ammunition to be released when he tried to extract it from his holster. It was a tragic mixup, with deadly results.

Brian's police radio was buzzing as a dispatcher in Winnipeg repeatedly called for an update. He grabbed the portable to respond.

"Down, member down. Get an ambulance RCMP detachment, get an ambulance at RCMP detachment at Russell. Member down," Brian yelled, his voice cracking as he struggled to catch his breath.

A full minute passed, and Brian remained alone, at his fallen partner's side. No signs of life, anywhere. Brian radioed in again, demanding help. The operator told him to hang on, that she was trying to find other police units. Brian considered driving Dennis to the hospital himself, but the operator said an ambulance would be there right away.

Suddenly, a figure appeared on the scene. Brent Havelanse had left the Russell curling club and was driving down Main Street, past the RCMP detachment, when he saw a police car race through the ditch, a truck in hot pursuit. Havelanse watched from a distance as the truck crash into the side of the police car, and immediately knew something was terribly wrong. He had turned towards the station, passing by the speeding truck as he drove through the main entrance and into the parking lot, where the police car had come to a stop.

Havelanse knew some of the RCMP officers in the area and wanted to make sure everything was okay. He quickly recognized the uniformed officer standing outside the damaged car as Brian Auger, a friend and occasional golf partner. Brian was yelling into his police radio, intense and upset. This was not the Brian he knew, the one who never got rattled no matter how much he was teased on the golf course.

Havelanse called out Brian's name, just as another police car pulled up. Brian was waving his arms, frantically, motioning the officer to hurry. Havelanse backed off, obviously in the way of something very important. He returned to his truck, concerned but figuring the police had things under control.

Const. Jennifer Pashe was also speeding to the scene, alone in her cruiser car, terrible thoughts racing through her mind. She had heard the breathless cries for help from the two men she was supposed to be having coffee with. She could sense the fear, the desperation, and the loneliness Dennis and

Brian must have been feeling, under siege, nobody around to help. As she had neared the detachment, she saw the flashing emergency lights of the police SUV in the distance, then watched a truck go speeding by her. She didn't try to stop it, her first priority was checking on her fellow officers. Jennifer first saw Brian, standing in the snow, arms in the air. The look on his face told her something terrible had happened.

Jennifer began scanning the scene, looking for Dennis. Her eyes stopped as they reached the inside of the shot-up cruiser car. There, in the passenger seat, his face down on the console, was Dennis.

Jennifer screamed at Dennis to get up. His lips appeared to move, and a finger or two on his right hand seemed to twitch, although she couldn't be sure. Dennis's face was dripping with blood, so Jennifer grabbed a blanket and gently wiped it away. She loosened the zipper on his winter jacket, thinking it might help him breathe. Brian stood by her side, helpless, going through the chaotic scene in his head over and over, and praying for the ambulance to get there soon. The operator was back on the radio.

"Which member is down?" she asked Brian.

"Strongquill," he replied in a solemn voice, surveying the grisly scene.

"Strongquill? Injuries?" she asked.

"I believe he's down," said Brian, taking a long, deep breath before speaking once again.

"One member's down."

The ambulance arrived minutes later, but Brian and Jennifer could see the obvious. Dennis hadn't made it. Four shots had pierced his upper body. The final shot proved to be fatal, tearing through his back as he twisted and turned in his seat, unable to escape because the crumpled metal of his passenger door had turned the RCMP cruiser into a tomb. Steel pellets had pierced his aorta, the largest blood vessel in the body, causing rapid bleeding and near instant death.

* * * * * *

Emotions were running high inside the stolen truck as it snaked its way through the back roads of western Manitoba. Robert had just scored the ultimate victory over the enemy, who had run away like cowards. *Those sorry motherfuckers.* But Robert's celebration was dampened by Danny, who was losing blood rapidly. The police officer had shot him straight through the right arm, while another bullet had pierced his back. His white shirt was crimson red.

Laurie was frantic, and Robert was trying to console his girlfriend, telling her everything would be all right. Danny continued driving north, no time to stop and switch drivers. They needed to find a place to stop, rest, recover. Robert knew police would be blanketing the area, but he wasn't worried. There were plenty more weapons and ammunition in the truck.

It was 1 a.m. when the truck pulled into a large yard just off Highway 264, near the western edge of Manitoba. They had driven for about 20 minutes, and there was no sign of any cops. Robert and Danny discussed their next move.

Police likely had a good description of their truck, so they would need to get new wheels, and fast. The brothers decided splitting up, at least for the moment, was the best option.

Larry Keller was sitting at his kitchen table, a bloody knife in one hand and a beaver carcass in the other. A successful day of trapping meant a long night of skinning and carving. His eyes were suddenly diverted off the task at hand when he saw the lights of a truck in his yard. Keller got up and walked out the front door, turning on the porch light. Instantly, the truck backed up and sped away.

Spooked by the sight of the homeowner, Robert, Danny and Laurie moved on looking for easier prey. They found it just up the highway, where another truck was parked in a driveway. Robert jumped inside, hot-wired it and was driving away within seconds, Laurie at his side. Danny continued on in the Silverado. Divide and conquer was the game plan.

* * * * * *

The late-night phone call jolted Rob Lasson out of bed. It was Sonny Richards, the officer in charge of Waywayseecappo.

"I don't know how to tell you this. I don't want to tell you this. Dennis was just shot and killed."

Rob was frozen. His thoughts turned immediately to Mandy, and Korrie, and the kids. Sonny paused for a second, then continued.

"If you can, go to Rossburn, grab all the shotguns you can, all the shells, and come and pick me up in Wayway," Sonny said sternly. All police units in the province were being called into action.

The thought of going to work now was too much to bear, but Sonny insisted it had to be done.

"We've got to pull ourselves together. We've got to go get these guys for Dennis. There will be time to cry later."

Rob collected himself, did as he was told, and drove through the blowing snow to pick up Sonny. Rob bristled as Sonny told him how Dennis had been ambushed, chased and then killed in cold blood. His gun had fallen apart and his door was smashed in. There had been nowhere to run.

"We have to stop these guys," said Sonny. "But I think someone else is going to die tonight. These guys are obviously desperate."

* * * * * *

Matthew Lavallee heard the tragedy play out over his police radio while working in the Roblin area. He was sickened to hear a fellow officer was down. Lavallee had tried to race to the scene in Russell, to answer Brian's desperate calls for help, but had to return to his police station when the gas pedal on his cruiser car kept sticking.

Now in a new vehicle, Lavallee was getting a second chance to help, as RCMP were setting up roadblocks throughout the western part of the province. RCMP in Saskatchewan had also been notified. Lavallee was posted at Highways 482 and 83, about 16 kilometres north of Russell. About 2 a.m., a truck appeared on the horizon, heading his way. It was followed closely by a second truck. Both appeared to be speeding up as they approached the roadblock. Lavallee's heart was racing, sensing these might be the suspects.

The two vehicles sped past him, making no attempt to stop. He gave chase, radioing to other officers he could be in pursuit of the suspects. Lavallee was several hundred metres behind as the chase wound its way through the Assiniboine Valley's sharp curves and steep drops. He kept the trucks in sight as they approached the top of a hill. They abruptly turned off Highway 482 and down a gravel road. Lavallee, who knew the area well, believed the suspects had just sealed their fate by turning down a dead end.

His cruiser car parked at the top of the hill, Lavallee waited anxiously for backup. Soon, Jennifer Pashe arrived.

She had just come from the grisly scene at Russell and wanted to help catch Dennis's killers. As the officers waited on the hill, suddenly, a single truck appeared, headed right at them, and once again the Silverado blew past without any trouble. Lavallee re-started the chase, but couldn't keep up, losing sight as they neared the Saskatchewan border. He had lost the cat-and-mouse game.

Rusty Spragg and a handful of other RCMP officers were parked on the Saskatchewan side of the border, in the tiny hamlet of Shellmouth, listening as Lavallee described a suspect truck possibly headed their way, believed to be the murder vehicle Lavallee said they were likely carrying the suspects wanted for killing Dennis Strongquill less than two hours earlier.

Sure enough, the truck appeared on the horizon, travelling at high speeds and racing towards the Saskatchewan officers. As they had done moments earlier, the occupants paid no attention to the officers, blowing by them. Spragg and his partner gave chase, but backed off when two loud gunshots were fired their way, from the suspect vehicle. One Mountie was already dead that night, and Spragg had no desire to be the second.

* * * * * *

The Sand brothers and Laurie were together again, now on a darkened stretch of road after leaving a trail of police in their wake, giving them yet another victory on what was proving to be quite a night. The trio had decided it was best to travel together, especially since Danny's condition was deteriorating and he didn't know how much longer he could drive. The Silverado, which they'd kept for days, would have to go. They were sitting ducks the longer they remained in it. But the brothers couldn't just leave it intact at the side of the road, given the evidence they'd likely leave behind. One look at the truck showed just how lucky they'd been. Robert counted several bullet holes in the driver's side door, which struck just below the window where Danny's head had been exposed.

With the strike of a match, the truck was lit up in seconds. They stole another nearby truck, a Ford, and drove away, leaving a red hot flame behind them. As they had done all along, they were sure to grab their Bible.

The sign at the side of the road said "Stockholm", and Danny told his brother to stop near the driveway to a farm up ahead. His gunshot wounds were causing tremendous pain, and he needed something for it, and fast. Danny prided himself on being tough, but this was nearly too much to bear.

Robert was growing weary, struggling to keep himself focused after blasting through two police roadblocks. He wondered about the route they were on. The snow-covered roads all seemed the same, but he was trying to avoid the main highways.

Laurie was also fighting sleep, constantly reassuring Danny things would be all right. At least, she hoped they would. Laurie promised to call her mom. Donna Bell, the nurse, would know what to do. Laurie just didn't know how she would explain the situation to her mom, and dreaded making the call.

Robert stopped the truck at the darkened farmhouse. Danny, clearly agitated, told his brother to drive up to the house immediately. Grabbing a shotgun, Danny crawled out and began prowling around the home while Robert and Laurie stayed inside the truck. Danny forced his way inside within seconds.

The floors creaking with his every step, Danny looked around for any signs of life but saw none. It appeared the residents had gone away for Christmas. Danny, desperate for something to stop his pain, began a hurried search through the kitchen cabinets and drawers, yelling and swearing and throwing items to the floor. He grabbed a television set in the kitchen, smashing it to the ground. At least that felt good.

Danny went downstairs, and destroyed another television, this time by firing a shotgun blast straight through the screen. Why should Robert get to do all the shooting? Back upstairs, Danny went through the master bedroom, and opened fire on a large mirror, smashing it into pieces.

Finally, Danny saw something he liked – alcohol. He grabbed a 12-pack of Brewhouse beer, immediately cracking one open, chugging it back and then smashing the bottle on the floor. He took the case to go. Danny also grabbed a mickey of rye, which he poured on his wounds to clean them. It stung like hell, but the pain was only temporary and certainly no worse then what he was already feeling.

Danny began rummaging through drawers, grabbing a gold bracelet with the name "Lawrence" engraved on it. He took another gold chain with a cross, which he wanted to give to Laurie. He also stole a DVD player, a black leather jacket and some chocolate bars, to keep their energy up. Danny finally left the home, which by now was in shambles, and returned to the truck outside.

It was early morning when Laurie picked up the cell phone and called her mother. Desperate times called for desperate measures.

Donna Bell was relieved to hear her daughter's voice, but sensed something was terribly wrong. Laurie said she didn't have long to talk. Donna's heart sank when Laurie said she was with Robert and Danny, who had been shot. Laurie said she wasn't looking for a lecture, just some help.

"You have to turn yourself in," a tearful Donna pleaded. Laurie said they were in too deep, had come too far, and had too much to lose. She hung up the phone.

* * * * * *

William Rees was in the middle of a deep sleep when his barking dog and the familiar sound of his truck running jolted him from bed. The clock said 5:20 a.m. Rees went to the window and saw an unfamiliar vehicle sitting in his driveway, lights on and running, the shadows of at least two people inside. Rees watched as a third figure left the truck and got inside his 1996 Dodge pick-up.

Rees threw on some clothes and rushed outside, just as his truck was pulling away, along with the mystery vehicle. He fumbled for his keys, finding one which fit another truck parked in the yard, and got in. After a few seconds of moaning and groaning from the frozen vehicle, Rees was on the road, in pursuit of the thieves.

He could see the two trucks ahead of him, and the distance appeared to be narrowing. Suddenly, they both pulled into a field, turning off their lights. An uneasy feeling came over Rees, as the thieves appeared to be baiting him. He considered his options, but decided to turn back towards home. There were three of them, and Rees decided safety was more important than property. As he began driving away, he jumped at the sound of a rifle shot bouncing off the back of his rear bumper. Rees sped up, knowing he had made the right decision.

Robert, Danny and Laurie, now behind the wheel of the 1996 Dodge, made one final-trade in as they continued to head

140

west through Saskatchewan. At 6:30 a.m., they upgraded to a 2002 Chevy S-10, which they found inside a closed garage, the keys still in the ignition. They drove straight through the garage door, heading back to the highway. Things were really going their way tonight!

* * * * * *

Morning was approaching, and Robert, Danny and Laurie knew the rising sun could blow the cover off what had been a wild night. They had to find shelter fast. The heavy snow was making it nearly impossible to see, and Robert was fighting to keep his eyes open and the truck on the right side of the road. Twice, he nearly veered into the path of oncoming semi-trailers. They entered the small Saskatchewan town of Grenfell and pulled into the only hotel they could see.

Gerald Edwards doesn't usually get new customers checking in at 6:40 a.m., nor does he often see someone walk in to rent a room with blood smeared on their face. Edwards was concerned, and balked when the bloodied, messy-haired visitor asked him for a room. Edwards, who had seen plenty of weirdos during his time behind the motel desk, had a bad feeling and falsely told the man he had no vacancies. In truth, many of the rooms were filled for a hockey tournament, but there were beds available. He suggested they go up the road, to a small town called Wolseley.

Robert knew his appearance was going to attract some strange looks, but that was the least of his worries right now. He and the gang drove on. He walked in to the Wolseley Motel, Danny's dried blood still caked on his face and hands.

He told the clerk, who identified himself as Jerry, that he had lost his identification, and that a friend had lent him a

141

truck when his broke down near the Manitoba border. The man agreed to give Robert a room, but Robert wasn't about to sign his real name. Instead, he wrote "Bill M. Wright" on the invoice, and gave the man a $100 bill – among the last of the money they had. Robert asked for an 11 a.m. wake-up call, and Jerry told him they could stay as late as they wanted, since business was slow.

Robert returned outside, helping Laurie and Danny unload the bags of weapons and other items in to suite five of the motel. It was tiny, with a single bed and little room to spare, but none of that mattered. The fugitives got inside, and immediately went to sleep – too tired to notice the motel was directly on the Trans Canada Highway, their bright red stolen truck standing in sharp contrast to the dreary white landscape now being exposed by the early-morning sun.

* * * * * *

Word of Dennis Strongquill's murder spread to police detachments across the country, officers of all stripes waking up on the morning of Friday, December 21 to the grim news. But in Manitoba and Saskatchewan, grief had to be put on hold while a huge task remained – catch the killers.

Descriptions of a string of stolen vehicles, including the burned-out truck used in the killing, were being broadcast across the land, with officers puzzled and frustrated that the suspects had got away. But by mid-morning, the break they had been waiting for came in the form of a phone call.

Jerry Olm, night clerk at the Wolseley Motel, heard about the murder just across the border, and was immediately suspicious of the strangers who had checked themselves in hours earlier. He called the RCMP, giving them a description of the man who had checked in, and the truck he was driving.

Lawrence Shier, a customs and excise officer in Saskatchewan, was driving down the Trans Canada when he heard a police radio broadcast about the truck parked outside suite five. He called police after confirming the vehicle was still there at 11 a.m. An officer with the area detachment asked him to remain outside the motel, at a safe distance, to ensure the truck didn't leave. The officer told Shier a large team of officers was quickly being assembled to converge on the motel.

* * * * * *

Robert was startled by the sound of pounding at the door. Still groggy, he stayed in bed while Danny answered the wake-up call he had requested only hours earlier. Danny was in agony, the bullet wounds still oozing blood. Today was his 21st birthday. But Danny wasn't in much of a mood to celebrate, pain masking any joy he might otherwise feel.

Laurie climbed in bed beside Robert, trying to rouse him from sleep. Robert didn't want to budge, and lounged in bed for some time.

Robert finally got out of bed about 1 p.m., and the trio began discussing their next move. Robert and Danny decided it would be easier to take Laurie home, back to her family in Athabasca. Laurie didn't agree, but the brothers didn't care. This was no time for arguments. They would head back west, leave Laurie in Alberta, then carry on to British Columbia where they could lay low, hide out with some friends. They would leave immediately.

Robert was just getting dressed when he heard a noise outside the room, the sound of several vehicles moving at once. He walked to the window, pulled aside the curtains, and felt his heart jump into his throat. There, parked on the Trans Canada, were two dark blue Suburbans. The police had found them.

* * * * * *

Darren Topping was one of 16 police officers summoned to the Wolseley Motel for the most important assignment of their lives. A comrade had been killed in the course of duty, and Topping was there to catch the killers. Positioned behind two police vehicles parked on the highway, about 70 yards north of the motel, he had a perfect view of the front of suite five. At exactly 2:24 p.m., police saw the first signs of life inside the room.

"We just observed what appears to be movement in the bottom left-hand corner of the door...of the window right next to the door," Topping's partner, Murray Chamberlain, said over the police radio.

"Roger. Copy. Movement bottom left-hand window, near the door," replied Bob Bazin, the staff sergeant in charge of the operation. He was situated at a command centre just up the highway, which had been shut down to traffic in either direction. All officers were told to hold their positions.

Desperation was growing inside suite five of the Wolseley Motel.

"We're gonna have to shoot out way out of here," Robert said to his brother, who nodded in agreement. If they were going down, the brothers were going to do it fighting.

Danny grabbed a high-powered rifle, while Robert reached for a shotgun. The brothers made sure their weapons were loaded. Robert told Laurie to remain inside the suite, to hide in the bathtub. Stubborn as always, she refused.

144

Robert used his feet to kick out the rear window and Laurie climbed out first, with Danny and Robert directly behind her.

Danny insisted on going up to the roof to get a better look, saying the couple cops they'd seen on the highway were likely all they were dealing with. After all, this was a small town, how much manpower could they really muster? Robert didn't like the idea, it was too dangerous. But Danny insisted, so Robert helped lift him up so he could grab hold of a ledge. Danny climbed on to the roof, bringing the rifle with him. Robert and Laurie remained on the ground, while Danny hurried over to a spot near a chimney. He briefly retreated after counting six officers in the distance, telling Robert and Laurie what they were facing.

"Stay low," Robert told Danny, who returned to the chimney area.

* * * * * *

Several members of an elite RCMP sniper team scattered around the Wolseley Motel. Bob Gourlay and Al Lukasewich nestled behind a stack of hay bales sitting in a farmer's field. Crouched on the ground, their hearts raced as they saw Danny climb to the roof, gun in hand.

"He's on the roof, somebody's on the roof," Gourlay said over the radio.

"He's by the chimney. He's got a gun," added Lukasewich.

Gourlay told the other officers they had a clear kill shot if needed.

On the other side of the motel, sniper Kelly Painter stood alone. He was livid, having tried several times to radio his colleagues about what he was seeing from his view atop a gas station. A malfunctioning police radio kept interrupting him every time he tried to tell them there was an armed man on the roof. Painter was increasingly concerned about the safety of the officers, who were all lower than Danny and in a vulnerable position.

Painter watched as Danny crept around the rooftop, taking a position at the chimney. Danny was down on all fours, peering through his scope, the gun aiming directly at the officers on the highway. Painter decided to act. He focused his rifle on Danny's head, and fired two quick shots.

Danny jumped at the sound of gunfire whizzing by his head. The shots were close, but neither hit him. Four more shots followed, as he stayed as close to the snowy rooftop as possible. Danny squeezed his gun tightly, sensing the end was near.

"Half a dozen shots fired from the subject!" Lukasewich yelled into his radio, believing Danny had opened fire on them.

Waiting this out was no longer an option for Gourlay.

"We're gonna take him out," he said, seeking permission from the operational commander.

"Go ahead. Over," Bazin replied without hesitation.

On the nearby rooftop, Painter was trying desperately to tell his fellow RCMP members about what he'd just done. But his radio still wouldn't allow him to broadcast messages. Painter could hear the confusion from the other members, believing Danny had just shot at them. He was powerless to stop the deadly chain reaction which followed.

Lukasewich took aim at Danny's head, and squeezed the trigger. The result was immediate. Danny crumpled to the roof, blood pouring from his head, into the snow.

"Badger's down on the roof, badger's down on the roof. He's not moving, he's not moving," Gourlay matter-of-factly informed all officers.

Robert, still standing in the nook with Laurie, was staring directly at his brother when the gunshot blew through Danny's skull, killing him instantly. Laurie unleashed a horrific scream. Robert yelled Danny's name, over and over. There was no response.

Laurie was crying, saying this had to end. A million emotions were running through Robert's head. He wanted to fight, but he couldn't comprehend what had just happened. His brother was dead. Faced suddenly with his own mortality, and Laurie's, Robert made a decision he never thought he could. It was time to give up, to surrender to the police, the enemy.

Robert put down his shotgun. Laurie, terrified and shaking, went first, slowly walking from the nook to the front of the motel, her hands raised straight up in the air. Robert followed seconds later, a slow, steady pace, straight into the arms of waiting police officers.

CHAPTER NINE

A dim light flickered inside the small Waywayseecappo RCMP station. Sgt. Sonny Richards, the head of the tight-knit detachment, brought his surviving members together, just hours after Dennis was gunned down in cold blood. He knew it was important to stick together, the brotherhood and sister-hood of police officers. Brian Auger was there, barely able to even look at, or speak with, his fellow officers. Everyone gave him the space he needed. Community elders had come to the police station, offering tobacco and leading the officers in traditional prayers – for themselves, and for Dennis.

Behind the detachment, anger boiled up inside Mandy Delorande, one she struggled to control. *They have taken his life, my life, our daughter's life,* she thought, still unable to process the news Dennis had been killed, just hours after they had played cards, shared a laugh, a hug, a kiss. *That was never supposed to be goodbye.* The police told her two suspects were in custody, a third was dead. Mandy, consumed by hatred, wished they were all dead.

* * * * * *

Sitting alone in the backseat of a police car, Laurie was cold, scared and confused. Separated from Robert for the first time in weeks, she struggled to sort out what had just happened, but it was all such a blur. Danny was dead, that much was certain. And Robert had just surrendered, not wanting to fight anymore, the horror of watching his brother die too much to bear. They had hit the end of their road. And how they got here suddenly didn't make any sense to Laurie.

Her eyes filled with tears, Laurie looked up to see a police officer walking towards the car, then get inside. It was a woman.

"Are you cold?" asked Const. Lana Marie Gregoire. Laurie, unsure of whether she should respond, simply nodded her head. The officer turned up the heat. A warm gust of air brushed gently against Laurie's face, and her tears began to dry.

Robert sat quietly in a separate cruiser, far apart from Laurie. His hands and feet were shackled tightly together, pinching off the circulation in his arms. The police car pulled away from the Wolseley Motel, up the Trans Canada highway to the RCMP detachment in nearby Indian Head, a sleepy little town where the arrival of two police killers would be the biggest local event in ages.

Robert kept playing the sight of his brother falling on the roof of the motel, never to get up again, over in his head. *That should have been me,* Robert thought to himself, clenching his hands, making a fist, struggling to control his rage. But Robert was no longer in a position to make decisions for himself. The enemy was, and he hated it.

Cold air, rushing in through a broken window, slapped Robert in the face. Just as he was being loaded into the car by swat team members, a police dog unit had suddenly backed up, hitting the passenger side and shattering one of the windows. Const. Melvin Zurevinsky was blasting the heat in the front seat. But none of it was reaching Robert.

* * * * * *

Elaine Sand and her son, Dusty, were returning to their Westlock, Alberta home on the evening of December 21 after running some errands. As they travelled down the long, snow-packed country road towards their house trailer, a police car appeared in the rear-view mirror, lights flashing. Elaine had become accustomed to the sight of police officers in recent days, with Robert and Danny both being on the run. *Maybe they have some good news,* Elaine thought.

Danny had been shot dead, while perched on a motel roof in Saskatchewan clutching a gun, the officer told Elaine. Robert was in custody, having given himself up. The girl, Laurie, was with him. Elaine began to wail, her knees shaking and her heart racing. She felt faint, and saw the shocked look in Dusty's eyes as she passed out in the front seat of her car.

* * * * * *

Robert knew there would be lots of questions from the police, and he was willing to give answers – at a price. More than anything, he wanted to see Laurie, to talk to her, make sure she was all right. He knew they were going to be apart for a while, maybe forever, and wanted one more night, just to hold and kiss her, tell her he loved her. Robert also wanted to speak to his mother, to tell her about Danny. She shouldn't have to find out from anyone else. Robert may not be in control anymore, but he still wielded some power, power he intended to use to his full advantage.

Jim Atras and Joe Nowell, two grey-haired and gruff major crime investigators with the RCMP, walked in to the Indian Head detachment. They had interrogated killers before, but never in a case which hit so close to home. They knew trust was the key – getting the killers to believe they had their best interests at heart, that they really cared, that they understood it was just a mistake. They did care – that these two cop killers were convicted and sent away for as long as possible. For Atras and Nowell, keeping their composure was going to be a struggle. But how they handled these next few hours would be critical. There was no room for error.

Robert slowly lifted his head as the two men entered the tiny interview room he had been sitting in for what seemed like hours. He was relieved they weren't wearing uniforms. It would be easier to deal with them that way. The officers introduced themselves, then checked over a video camera in the room, turning it on. Robert took the initiative.

"Umm...I would like to make a phone call, to let my mother know. I don't know if she knows or not. I really don't care what happens to me. Like, whatever you guys want to know, I'll let you know but I have things that I want, because...I don't know. Not everybody knows but I...I have spots of my lungs and I don't...want to go see a doctor. I would like to spend some time with fiancée 'till I'm...I don't know if this is possible or not, but 'til tomorrow morning, 'til we leave. I'll give you guys whatever you want to know. I just want to make a phone call and, spend the night with her. And then come Monday morning, we'll do whatever," Robert told the men.

Atras had expected this, and knew playing to a criminal's needs and wants was an effective way of doing business.

"Ok, Robert, this is how we have to work this, okay? We can't promise you anything right now. If you want to make a phone call, we'll take you to a telephone and you can make a phone call. That's your right. You can call whoever you want," he said.

Robert was filled with a sense of relief. Elaine would be worried sick.

Then the other shoe dropped.

"If I get this correctly, you want to spend the night with your girlfriend tonight?" Atras said.

"If she'll have me," replied Robert.

This was certainly a novel request, the officers thought.

"We…no, we can't do that because that's against policy. And that's the rules that I did not make up and we can't a male and female people in the same cell, Robert. I'm sorry. I had nothing to do with that. We can't…we can't do that for you," said Atras.

Robert's blood began to boil. The police could do anything they wanted. Since when do the rules mean anything, he thought. Robert demanded the officers tell him who was in charge.

Atras could feel the power struggle in the room, and wasn't about to back down.

"Well, it's not a matter of outranking. It's just policy. And it doesn't matter what rank you are, we can't…we can't break that policy. I'm sorry about that," he said.

Nowell could see the interview was getting off to a bad start and jumped in to help his partner.

"We're not gonna try to trick you…. We're not gonna let you think that you're gonna get to spend some time with your girlfriend and then blindside you and say, oops, sorry, we lied. Too bad, so sad, pal. I'm telling you straight up, we can't do that part," said Nowell.

Atras wanted to change the subject, and fast.

"Now you wanted to talk to us. What did you want to tell us there, Robert. I know what happened," he said.

Robert no longer felt like cooperating, not when these assholes wouldn't even let him see Laurie. Instead, they were feeding him bullshit about policy.

Atras and Nowell were quickly losing control of the situation, before Robert had even uttered a single word about murdering Dennis. Nowell began to pour on the charm, with Atras following his lead.

"What's done is done, buddy. Can't go back in time," said Nowell. Calling Robert Sand his buddy sickened Nowell, but he was doing his job. Just like Dennis Strongquill had been doing his job. Only look where it got him.

"Robert, we're sorry what happened, the way things have turned out, especially about your younger brother. Unfortunately, we can't go back, as much as we…you would like to," said Atras, who knew where his partner was going with the conversation.

"We'd like to take back a few days, wouldn't we. Maybe change a few things?" Nowell continued.

"Would you like to tell us what happened, Robert? Start right from the very beginning," said Atras. He wanted Robert to quit stalling.

A million thoughts were racing through Robert's head. He *did* want to talk, to get things off his chest. But he wanted to do it on his terms. Robert couldn't get his mind off Laurie, and his mother, who would be home, waiting for word on her boys. Finally, the officers took him to call Elaine.

Robert was placed in a small room with a telephone, but his mother's voice only added to his pain. Elaine was a wreck, crying and screaming. Dennis Sand was at her side, trying to console his wife. Things had played out just as Dennis had feared. All their hopes and dreams of a brighter future for their boys were gone.

"I am sorry Mom," Robert kept repeating, tears forming in his blood-shot eyes.

He hated hearing his mother like this, and felt responsible for her pain. "Sorry" just didn't do it. He told Elaine he loved her and promised to call again soon. Robert hung up the phone, then buried his head in his hands, sobbing.

* * * * * *

Atras and Nowell were waiting in the interview room when Robert returned. While he had been on the phone, the two officers had discussed his proposal to see Laurie. Worried this could hold up the interview, they agreed to bring Laurie into the room, as long as the video camera kept rolling and they remained as well. This was unprecedented, and potentially dangerous, but Atras and Nowell knew this was no ordinary interrogation. A police officer had been killed, and if bringing his killers to justice meant bending the rules, or throwing them out altogether, so be it.

Nowell had started a pot of coffee, and asked another officer to grab some cigarettes. They would be here a while. Better make sure they were comfortable. Robert was impressed with how the officers were treating him and began to ease up, to let his guard down, to peel away the layers of his mask.

"Sorry about this whole mess," said Robert, again feeling the word sorry just didn't measure up.

"Hey, one step at a time, buddy," replied Nowell.

Robert was thrilled at the opportunity to see Laurie. She must be so confused, so afraid. Was she mad at him? Robert had to know. Before she came in, Nowell warned Robert he could not discuss the case, in any way, or else the visit would be terminated. Robert was willing to do anything if it meant seeing Laurie. His handcuffs were removed.

Laurie walked into the room, wearing jeans and a baggy sweatshirt that seemed to swallow her tiny frame. Robert, seated on a couch across from the door, perked up, his eyes meeting hers. She grabbed him in a warm embrace. It felt so good to be loved, and needed, Robert thought. Laurie was crying, and Robert was fighting tears himself. Atras and Nowell sat stone-faced in the corner.

"I love you," Laurie whispered in Robert's ear. These were the words he wanted to hear. Nothing else mattered for as long as this moment lasted.

The pair continued talking in hushed voices, not wanting the officers to hear them, but the video camera picked up nearly every word and gesture. Laurie mentioned their engagement, saying she was worried what would become of it. Robert said he'd called his mother, and that his parents would let Laurie come live with them, once the police let her go, if her own family didn't want her back. Robert knew he was going down, but planned on his confession setting Laurie free. After all, he was the one who had pulled the trigger.

Atras and Nowell continued making small talk, made uncomfortable by the scene unfolding before them. The sight of Dennis's killers necking and laughing was enough to make them sick. But business was business. Nowell asked Robert what he took in his coffee, promptly serving up the two sugars and a cream he ordered.

"I'm trying so hard not to cry," said Laurie, as Robert held her tightly in his arms.

"I'll get transferred back to Edmonton. You can come see me there," Robert told her.

He began worrying about what Laurie's mother thought of him. "Did you call your mom?" he asked.

"Yeah," said Laurie.

"Is she worried?"

"Yeah, she couldn't sleep a wink."

"Is she mad at me for being stupid?"

"No," Laurie said, without hesitation. "She's really con-fused...really scared. She's really worried," she continued.

Atras and Nowell had seen and heard just about enough.

"I don't want to be a party pooper here, but in fairness, we should start to wind down. So why don't we have another cigarette and finish our coffee, okay?" Nowell said.

Laurie and Robert continued to stare into each other's eyes, making jokes about their unsightly appearances following weeks on the run and too many hours without sleep. Laurie said she liked Robert's shirt. She pointed out that his hair was greasy.

"Okay, folks. We gotta move on now," said an increasingly disturbed Nowell, who wanted to turn the conversation back to the real issue.

It was 8:54 p.m. The stomach-churning visit had lasted nearly half an hour.

Laurie asked for one more hug. Robert gratefully obliged, not wanting to let go. Finally, they parted. Laurie was taken away and Robert was once again alone with the two officers.

* * * * * *

Nowell was a little nervous, fearing Robert was going to renege on the deal now that he'd seen Laurie. Maybe he'd try to play them for more – another call, another visit, some kind of deal? Atras wasted no time, telling Robert to begin with his story.

"I have a question," Robert began. "I'm going to give you a statement. It's gonna convict me on numerous things. I'll…I'll tell you all kinds of shit. I'll fuck you guys right up. But I was wondering, when I go to court, is there a chance I can plead down?"

The officers had been expecting this.

"You can do anything you want to do when you go to court. You can handle it any way you want to handle it, okay?" said Nowell. "We're not gonna…we're not gonna try to sewer you here on everything under the sun. We're not gonna try to trick you on anything else. For now, let's just deal."

Robert sensed he had taken this as far as he could. There was no use delaying it any longer. He began to talk, knowing what he said would determine not only his future, but Laurie's as well. He chose his words carefully, speaking slowly, avoiding eye contact with the officers. His delivery was completely deadpan, devoid of the emotion and chaos they had felt on the snowy highway that night.

"It started in Yorkton. We woke up that morning from a hotel room. We headed east, no particular destination. We were equipped with numerous firearms. I had shotguns, rifles, small calibre, high calibre. Uh, let's see. I think by the time we left Yorkton we were…I was pretty intoxicated. As you probably noticed with my fiancée, she drinks lots of sugar in her coffee. She's a recovering speed addict. I've cleaned her up but she still sleeps a lot, drinks a lot of sugar. So by the time we hit Manitoba, she was already asleep," said Robert.

He knew it was important to keep Laurie out of this entirely. With Danny dead, who else was there to blame? He continued talking.

"We went into a bar, all three of us. We decided to leave the bar 'cause my fiancée was pretty drunk. We got in the truck.

We drove around town for a little bit. She passed out and my little brother made a decision to keep heading east. We started heading east on some highway. I have no idea where. Um…had a car approach us from behind. When the car turned down its light…my little brother was driving and I told him to pull over. When we pulled over I stepped out of the passenger side with a 12-gauge sawed-off, three-inch magnum, I believe," he said.

Robert was replaying the incident in his head, in slow motion, but his pace began to quicken.

"I jumped out. I started shooting four rounds into the front of the vehicle. The vehicle backed up. I jumped in the truck. We pursued the vehicle, the police car. He turned into a town. I'm not even sure where. Um, when he pulled into town I can't remember if I shot while he was still driving but he pulled in front of the police detachment, isn't it?" he said.

Atras and Nowell were furiously scribbling notes, stunned by what they were hearing. Atras confirmed to Robert that the shooting occurred in front of the Russell RCMP station.

"And then I jumped out," Robert continued. "I kept shooting. I emptied six more rounds, I think, to the side of the police vehicle. We then proceeded to back up. We took off south, out of town, I believe. We passed a police car on the way out. I remember that. We were so freaked out. We started on some back roads. We were driving. My fiancée woke up briefly and I requested she go back to sleep. Everything was all right. We were on some back roads, looking for a new vehicle."

Robert recounted the string of stolen vehicles, his shooting at another police car on the roadblock, and their journey into Saskatchewan. He wanted another cigarette, which Nowell quickly provided.

"I got a hotel room where my younger brother was shot. We slept there for awhile because my brother was injured because he received two bullet wounds from the night before. Uh…when, uh…" Robert was having difficulty finishing his story. He couldn't clear the sight of Danny falling from his mind.

"We woke up. I was getting dressed. I looked out the window. I seen two swat units or whatever sitting on the highway. I looked out the back and there was swat around back. So we loaded up a couple of firearms. We jumped out the window, went around the back. The police said something; then shot. My little brother went up on the roof to look around. Then I heard a shot that wasn't one of our weapons. I called to my little brother. I seen him fall. I…I remember Laurie screaming. I remember telling her she had nothing to do with what happened the night before 'cause she still wasn't sure what happened. She gave herself up. I…called to my brother a few more times. Then I made the decision to come out unarmed. Because I felt I had to tell my parents what happened."

Robert paused to take a breath and collect his thoughts. He continued, machine-like in his delivery and with a steely glare in his eyes.

"It's so weird. If I wasn't engaged to Laurie, I would have come out shooting. I was…I was so mad when my brother fell. I didn't even know that the officer had been killed. I just…should have been me that fell, not him," said Robert, taking another deep breath and a drag of his cigarette.

"Do you guys have any questions?"

Atras and Nowell were shocked by the admission, realizing this could have been an even bigger bloodbath.

* * * * * *

Atras wanted to slow things down, to take Robert back to the beginning, and work out some of the smaller details. He knew that would be important in court, to get a complete picture, not to leave anything out. The veteran officers would stay all night if necessary. There weren't going to be any mistakes or oversights. Robert Sand would be brought to justice.

Robert was frustrated about having to tell the story over again. It had been hard enough to do the first time. He spent another hour describing their days on the run – the bank robbery, the stolen cars, the arsons, the break-ins.

Atras, who had heard a lot of confessions in his long career, was moved to ask a simple question.

"Why?"

"Because I was scared. I...like I told Joe, eh? I don't know how much longer I have to live. I don't know. My life is feeling pretty good. I have a fiancée. I was being stupid," said Robert. He knew the answer didn't make any sense, but he didn't know how else to describe something he was struggling to understand himself.

Atras asked the question again, not satisfied with the response.

"I was angered, I guess. My life was looking good. I didn't want to go back to jail. I just wanted to go and live somewhere by an ocean and have a family with my fiancée and I don't know...grow a garden or something," said Robert.

The officers were speechless. Dennis Strongquill was dead because of a garden? This was almost more than they could handle. Atras and Nowell continued firing a barrage of questions, shifting the focus to Laurie's involvement. Robert knew what they were trying to do, and he wasn't going to play their game. He repeatedly told them she was asleep, had no role in the case, and should be released.

The officers knew they had more than enough to put Robert away for murder. In some small sense, they appreciated Robert's honesty, but they also reeled at the chilling, matter-of-fact way he was able to describe what happened.

"We want to find out what happened and you want to clear the air and I think…and I think that's darn good what you're doing," said Nowell.

Robert interjected.

"What I want is to live on the ocean somewhere," he said.

"Well,, hey…hey, you've got a whole life ahead of you and we'll see whatever problems you have medically, whatever, we'll take on step at a time, okay," said Nowell, who continued to treat Robert with kid gloves despite the confession which had already flowed. "You're just going through a bad time right now, okay. And that's the bottom line and that's the only way to look at it, okay?"

Robert was surprised at how easy his words had come, how comfortable he felt with these two police officers, men he was supposed to hate..

"I am so worried, Joe. I've never done this. I mean give a statement," said Robert.

"Well, there's a first for everything. That's the bottom line," Nowell replied.

"That's what they say. Someone's gotta try everything at least once. That way when they die they're not sitting there going, I wish I would have done that. I'd rather be saying I wish I wouldn't have done that," said Robert.

The officers told Robert he had taken a positive step by confessing, but Robert only felt alone, and lost.

"I've never been married, never had a kid," he told the officers, sadness in his voice.

"Ah, you still got lots of time," said Nowell, making his best attempt to sound sincere.

Atras motioned for his partner, wanting to speak with him outside the interview room. Robert was nervous, but the officers said they were just had to go over a few things privately.

Outside the room, Atras and Nowell discussed their next move. They knew they had a slam-dunk with Robert, but were worried about the case against Laurie. The officers had poured on the bullshit, but felt they'd come up short where Laurie was concerned. Unlike Robert, who had declined an offer to speak with a lawyer, Laurie had refused to talk, instead wanting to see counsel. Robert was their only hope.

* * * * * *

As he sat alone in the room, Robert went over parts of the conversation and wondered if he had done good by Laurie. He had made sure to stress she was drunk, and asleep. Surely the police would have to let her go. When the officers returned to the room, the clock said nearly 10 p.m.

"Just a question. Being how Laurie was asleep for pretty much everything that happened...what does that mean for her?" asked Robert.

"We would like to talk to her about what happened but we can't go into it...into too much detail with you right now. Of course we have to speak to her about what happened and that's part of the investigation but we'll discuss this perhaps later, okay?" said Atras.

"But on that note, and we still are on tape, my mind if Laurie's done nothing, then Laurie is not responsible for anything, okay. That is straight goods," added Nowell.

Robert wanted to believe him, but history had taught him otherwise. Robert asked for another coffee.

The officers asked a final few questions, tying up some loose ends, but Robert wasn't budging when it came to Laurie.

"I wish we could have met under different circumstances, buddy," Atras told Robert.

"Chances are we wouldn't have," Robert said bluntly. "I'm just sorry our paths crossed this way. You never know. Might have met at a bar…"

"Had a beer," Atras said, interrupting.

Robert was feeling sorry for himself, and the officers could see it, and tried to capitalize on it.

"Let's just deal with what we have here and move forward. Like you said, you want to have kids. You want to get married," said Nowell.

"Can't do it now," said Robert.

"Why can't you? There's visitation. There's all that shit. You know that. Come on," said Nowell, seeing another glimmer of hope that Robert might open the door to Laurie.

"Yeah, but I know my girl and she probably won't give a statement and then they'll nail her just for being with us," said Robert.

"No, no, no, no. It ain't gonna happen if she's done nothing wrong. And that's the straight goods," said Nowell. "Let's just be honest with each other and it ain't gonna happen, okay? It is not gonna happen. If she's done nothing wrong and we don't think she's done anything wrong…You know what she's done wrong?" he asked.

"She was with me," said Robert.

"She was in the wrong place at the wrong time," said Nowell.

"She fell in love with me," said Robert.

"Yeah? And you guys happened to go on a binge and got all fucked up and out of whack. That's what went wrong," said Nowell.

"It wasn't supposed to be a binge," said Robert.

"Well, it ended up being something. And it's like, holy fuck! What have we fuckin' done?" said Nowell.

The officers wanted to end the interview. It was late, and they had hit a homerun. They thanked Robert again. Robert joked that he could make them famous. He actually liked these two guys, who had listened to him, for once, and actually seemed to care.

"No, no. We don't want to get famous this way, Robert. Don't say that. We'd rather just go on doing what we're doing," Atras said.

"You guys are different," Robert said.

"No, we just got a chance to know each other. That's what it is," said Nowell.

"Somebody died and then somebody else died and it compounds it, so what's the priority. We can't bring these people back. We have to deal with it and move on."

"Yeah, the wrong people died," said Robert.

The camera was turned off. The interview was over.

* * * * * *

Draped with a red and white Canadian flag, the bullet-riddled body of Dennis Strongquill was marched past his six children, police officers from across the country and shocked members of the community who had gathered on this mid-winter day to pay tribute to their fallen hero. It was two days after Christmas.

A dozen Manitoba RCMP officers, wearing their red serge uniforms, solemnly walked into the Powerview church, carrying his coffin on their broad shoulders. A small choir sang *Amazing Grace*.

More than 350 police officers in full uniform, many who had come from detachments across Canada and the United States, followed behind, forming an honour guard. Most had to wait outside the packed church, forming a line along the street. Off to the side, Brian Auger stood, clutching Dennis's Stetson in his hands. He cried softly, keeping his head lowered.

Dennis's eldest daughter, Teresa, was moved to tears as she approached the podium to speak. She had been thinking for days about what to say, about how to honour a man who had done so much for so many, inspired her to be loving and friendly and funny. The words flowed easier than she had expected.

"Dad was very proud of all his children and the RCMP, the two major loves of his life," said Teresa. Her brothers, Ricky and Joey, stood stoically beside her.

"Ultimately our dad was a hero. He loved his job and probably wanted to go this way. Our dad sacrificed himself fighting crime."

Teresa, standing in front of the mourners, vowed to carry on her father's legacy by returning to school next year to get her bachelor of nursing degree.

"I will devote my life to caring for people. Because like you, dad, I'm an excellent caregiver. Next time we meet, you will be proud," she said.

Gabriel Boulette told the congregation how Dennis had convinced him to join the RCMP when they first met in Powerview more than 15 years before. The pair had become great friends, and when Boulette got married, Dennis stood by his side as his best man. Now, he was carrying Dennis to his final resting spot.

"Dennis got me into the RCMP. He'd push you along. He gave me the confidence," he said.

"When I first thought of joining, I figured it was a long shot, but Dennis stepped in and gave me a little guidance. This is a big loss to us all. I'm losing a great friend."

RCMP chaplain Ed Kosa told mourners to search for strength.

"A death such as Dennis's shocks and saddens us all. Hold those memories very precious because those are Dennis's gifts to us," he said.

The service ended 75 minutes after it began, with a traditional Aboriginal song which spoke of Dennis rising up on an eagle's wings. A dozen native men began drumming and chanting a steady beat as pallbearers walked his coffin out of the church. A police piper took over, playing a subdued version of *Auld Lang Syne.*

Brian walked over to the coffin placing the Stetson on top, a final tribute to the man he'd watch die.

* * * * * *

"Bosom" was buried the following day, December 28, a quiet, private ceremony in Barrows which brought out several hundred mourners, including many of the same grieving police officers. His son, Joey, hung a pair of boxing gloves beneath the towering pine tree where his dad's body was laid to rest. Several wind chimes provided a sad musical backdrop.

In the summer, Mandy would plant daffodils around the gravesite, just like she and Dennis had around their home. For now, several large floral wreaths were placed in the snow.

Just a short walk away were the gravestones of about 30 of Barrows' lost residents, most of them young, most of them dead from unnatural causes. The cemetery, barely 50 years old, was filled with tragic tales of lost opportunities.

A young woman, running down the train tracks just outside of town, who slipped and fell, accidentally slitting her own throat with a wine bottle that broke after tumbling from her hands.

A teen, ostracized by the community after he flipped his car and killed a young passenger, who shot himself in the stomach when he couldn't stand being called "killer" anymore.

A man blown to pieces while working in a scrap metal yard, after a supposedly spent military shell exploded in his face.

A 21-year-old man shot to death by his own father, while trying to prevent the man from killing his mother.

A teen boy who killed himself by trying a rope around his neck, attaching the other end to a tree, and then got on the back of a horse and told it to giddy-up. His head was pulled off.

Dennis had planned to spend his golden years in Barrows, with Mandy and the kids, enjoying late-night card games, marshmallow roasts and campfire sing-songs. Dennis had indeed come home – but not on his terms.

CHAPTER TEN

First degree murder. No matter how much they heard it repeated – by their lawyers, their parents, the media – it didn't get any easier for Robert and Laurie to accept. Thirty years ago, the punishment would have been death. Now, it was life in prison with no parole for 25 years, a fate Robert equated with death. Manitoba was going after them to the full extent of the law. No plea bargains to be made, no deals to be had, no mercy.

Crown attorney Bob Morrison, a bright star in Manitoba's legal system, was given the biggest case of his career only days after the body of Dennis Strongquill had been laid to rest. He had read the papers, heard the television and radio reports, and felt the anger and outrage throughout his home province and the country. Morrison was always game for a challenge, and never shied away from hard work. He had stared down some of the most ruthless criminals in recent Manitoba history and made them pay. He would accept nothing less here. The weight of a province, of the entire police profession, was on his shoulders. But more importantly, he was carrying the burden for Dennis's six children, for Mandy Delorande, other loved ones, and for Brian Auger. He wouldn't let them down.

Morrison had two ways he intended to make his case, which was set to begin in April 2003 and would last eight weeks. The Criminal Code would be his greatest weapon. Federal politicians had decreed that the murder of an on-duty police officer was automatically first-degree murder, no questions asked, provided the killer knew the victim was a cop. If the flashing police lights, highway checkstop and ambush outside the Russell RCMP station couldn't convince a jury that Robert Sand knew exactly what he was doing and who he was shooting at, Morrison didn't know what would.

The other scenario to fall back on was that Dennis's killing had been planned and pre-meditated. To prove this, Morrison would use Robert's own words against him. The diary entry where he vowed the next officer he met would be a 'sorry motherfucker' was powerful evidence. A complete, two-hour videotaped confession didn't hurt the Crown's chances, either, nor did the truckload of stolen guns. As for motive, there was the obvious need to avoid arrest at all costs.

No, the case against Robert wasn't keeping Morrison up at night, but the one against Laurie was cause for concern. Her role in the killing was somewhat unclear. Robert claimed in his statement she slept through the entire attack, which Morrison found laughable. Robert had obvious reason to lie, to protect the woman he said he loved, and Morrison thought the jury would see right through him. However, the onus was on the Crown to prove she knowingly committed or was a party to murder and that was going to be tough. But then a woman named Rose Ferguson entered the picture.

* * * * * *

It was April 2003. Robert's day of reckoning was drawing near, and he was furious that his parents were thinking of coming to Brandon, Manitoba, where the trial was being held. Russell was too small, and Winnipeg was too far away, so the decision to hold the trial in Brandon was most logical. This blue-collar city, once known for wheat and now known for pork processing facilities, had hosted big trials before, but never of this magnitude. Home to some 40,000 people, the Dennis Strongquill murder trial would quickly become the talk of the town.

For Robert, the past 16 months in jail had been long and lonely. Robert had rarely spoken to anyone, shutting most of his family and friends out of his life. In August 2002, eight months after his arrest, he wrote one of the most difficult letters of his life, to former girlfriend Elisabeth Colbourne. He kept it short and sweet, telling her he wanted everyone in his life to just forget about him, to move on.

Robert had stayed in touch with his parents, and his brother, Dusty, but only by telephone. Now, Elaine said she and Dennis were thinking of coming out for the trial.

"Mom, people are going to be mean to you. They'll be spitting on you, yelling at you. I don't want you to go through that," Robert said during one of the brief calls he was allowed from Brandon Correctional Institute.

Elaine knew coming out for the trial would be a nightmare, and the prospect of facing Dennis Strongquill's family was too difficult to think about. What would she say? What could she say? Her heart went out to the family, which had been left shattered by the actions of her own two sons. Reluctantly, Elaine and Dennis agreed to stay put in Westlock.

But before she hung up, Elaine didn't waste the opportunity to tell her son what she was feeling.

"If it wasn't for Laurie, you wouldn't be there," she said.

Robert was quick, and defiant, with his response. "That's not true mom."

Robert filled his days, which were mostly spent in segregation, reading, writing and thinking. Prison guards told Robert that being isolated from other inmates was partly for his own protection. Robert begged to be released into the general population, telling the guards he didn't need their help. He could take care of himself. Hadn't he already proven that?

Robert didn't help his cause during the summer of 2002 when he attacked two guards taking him to court from his Brandon cell. The prison called it an escape attempt, but Robert didn't really think he would get away that day, or any day. He just didn't like their attitude, and wanted to send a message. There wasn't much thinking involved. Robert just acted.

* * * * * *

Laurie had never spent this long in jail, 16 months now, and it was pure torture. To help pass the days, she had kept her lines of communication open, speaking frequently with her mother and planning for a future that might never come. Laurie was young, small and pretty – those who knew her, and cared for her, worried she was an easy target for some of the more seasoned inmates.

Laurie quickly learned jailhouse relationships, superficial and formed by circumstance, didn't last long. Faces would come and go quickly, the familiar clank of a steel door signalling the exit of one inmate or the new arrival of another. Laurie was one of the rare exceptions. She was in custody, possibly forever, and literally fought to build a reputation as someone not to be messed with. She drove home the point during the summer of 2002 during the jailhouse beating of a new inmate who had abused her children. In the unique pecking order of prison, a child abuser was not welcome, lower than dirt, and deserving of anything that comes her way. Laurie and several other women acted as an unofficial welcoming committee, putting a beating on the woman, throwing a cup of urine as the ultimate insult, before the fight was finally broken up. Laurie had been charged with the incident, but that was besides the point. She had finally earned some respect.

Laurie made friends quickly, and formed relationships with several of her cellmates. One of those women, Rose Ferguson, came into Laurie's life shortly after her arrest. Laurie was slow to warm up to Ferguson, an Aboriginal woman who had just been arrested after returning to Canada from the United States. Ferguson had come home to face an old charge of stabbing her common-law husband, J.D. Laurie heard a lot about J.D. during the time she and Ferguson spent together, smoking cigarettes and talking about their predicaments, Laurie began to open up to her new cellmate. Although Ferguson was much older, Laurie soon bonded with her.

Ferguson spoke often about her children, her family, and the mistakes she'd made in life. Laurie, in turn, spoke about her own family, her love for Robert, and the tragic case which had landed her in prison. But just as quickly as she came into her life, Ferguson was gone, overnight it seemed. Her criminal charges were dropped weeks after her arrest, and she was free to leave. It was an emotional goodbye, and Laurie figured she had seen the last of Ferguson. She couldn't have been more wrong.

* * * * * *

Robert and Laurie's relationship suffered, their bond tested by distance and isolation. Robert was being held in Brandon,

Laurie in a Portage la Prairie women's jail. The towns were only 75 kilometres apart, but they may as well have been on opposite ends of the world. Their only time together came during a handful of routine court appearances leading up to the trial, where they could exchange knowing winks and glances and smiles, not caring who saw. But they would leave court wondering what the other was thinking, where they stood. There were more questions than ever, and no way to get the answers.

As the start of the trial drew near, the couple was able to see more of each other. Their defence lawyers had a series of legal motions and challenges which offered little hope, but at least gave them an opportunity to be in the same room, if only for a few hours, separated by sheriff's officers, steel handcuffs and shackles.

Funded by the public purse, Robert had his pick of the legal litter. He chose Greg Brodsky, one of Manitoba's most successful and well-known defence lawyers, who has tried more murder cases in Canada than anyone else. Brodsky didn't need this case to build a name for himself. He had already done that, representing some of the most infamous local killers during a career that had earned him more enemies than friends. With a licence to also practise in Ontario, Brodsky had even done some work on behalf of notorious sex killer Paul Bernardo. But Brodsky showed no signs of a man who had trouble sleeping at night in the upscale Winnipeg home he shared with his wife. He was just doing his job, and he happened to be damned good at it. Brodsky knew this case, more than any other he'd handled during his career, would be a real fight to get anything less than first-degree for Robert. The public demanded justice, and Robert's own words and actions would help them get it.

Laurie had hired defence lawyer Brian Midwinter, a big fish in the small pond of Brandon but a relative no-name on the wider criminal circuit. Midwinter lacked high-profile trial experience, but Laurie didn't care. She had first met him after her arrest, when the court assigned a representative from Legal Aid to speak with her, and the pair had hit it off. She saw no reason to change to a flashier lawyer with a bigger name, although it had nothing to do with price. The province was paying for her defence, just like Robert's, and the price tag would be high – nearly half a million dollars by the time the case was over. No, Midwinter was easy to get along with, listened well, and was just what Laurie wanted.

Robert and Laurie knew the difficult battle they were facing, but it got a lot tougher for Laurie when Midwinter told her a "star" witness had fallen in the Crown's lap – Rose Ferguson. Her former cellmate had told quite a story to police, claiming Laurie openly bragged about killing the RCMP officer, even admitting she cheered Robert on while he squeezed the trigger. Ferguson had become a jailhouse informant, and Laurie now worried her fate had been sealed.

The Crown cut no deals with Ferguson, but knew her testimony would come with a flood of legal warnings which could lead the jury to dismiss her entirely. Too many Canadian trials had been burned by bad informant evidence, and judges were now under strict orders to use extreme caution when allowing them to testify. Ferguson had the green light to take the stand, but whether the jury believed her remained to be seen.

Laurie was livid after hearing the woman she had once confided in, had trusted, had turned against her. The Crown was betting the farm on Ferguson's evidence, which contradicted everything Robert had said about a sleeping Laurie's lack of involvement.

* * * * * *

Brodsky, true to form, drew the ire of the public and police across Canada by launching a pre-trial motion that argued the life of a police officer was no more valuable than that of a regular citizen. He even downplayed the role of some officers and questioned how dangerous their job really was, noting some participate in the Musical Ride, a travelling RCMP horse show. Brodsky wanted to cut off the Crown's avenue of proving first-degree murder on the police issue alone, even if he drew the wrath of society in the process. He hadn't carved out an illustrious career by playing Mr. Nice Guy.

An outraged Canadian Police Association hired prominent Manitoba lawyer Hymie Weinstein to defend their interests during a heated court hearing. It was a moot point, as the judge quickly shot down the controversial motion. John Menzies could feel the pulse of the community, but had to put that aside in making his decision. It wasn't difficult, as courts in several other provinces had already ruled on the issue, paving the way, and giving Menzies an easy road to follow.

Menzies was also given the results of a defence team poll, which suggested the majority of Brandon residents felt Robert Sand and Laurie Bell were guilty as charged. The defence team used the poll to argue the case shouldn't be held in Brandon, where emotions would surely be running high. Menzies, a Brandon resident himself, threw out the motion. He knew picking a jury of 12 unbiased citizens might be difficult, but it wasn't impossible.

Robert and Laurie did score two major victories just before the trial began. First, they won a court ruling from Menzies which allowed their handcuffs (but not leg irons) to be removed when they sat in court. Robert especially hated the restraints, which were always tight on his wrists, especially since he had scrapped with the jail guards the previous summer. It wasn't in his nature to complain, knowing it wouldn't do any good. He let his lawyers do the work, and the judge ruled they could come off for the trial, despite strident opposition from Morrison, who warned the court was inviting another escape attempt, or something even more dangerous.

The second victory was a personal one, one that their lawyers weren't even aware of. During one court appearance, the couple managed to speak to each other from their prisoner's boxes, enough to devise a system where they would begin leaving letters for each other in the exercise yard at Brandon Correctional Institute. In anticipation of the trial beginning, and thanks to the vicious assault in Portage, Laurie had been moved to Brandon, where she was housed in the women's ward. She and Robert were being kept apart, but they still would be using the same facilities, just at separate times. They discussed plans for a secret drop-off spot, that only they would know about.

* * * * * *

On a crisp, clear spring morning, when much of the country was still sleeping off an overdose of turkey and stuffing from Easter Dinner, the city of Brandon was all business. Months of waiting were finally over, and the trial everybody was talking about had finally arrived. Robert and Laurie had been dreading this day, fearing the result may be a forgone conclusion. But there was no way to stop it. Their fate was out of their hands.

Morrison, a natural showman, had spent months preparing for the case, visiting every small Prairie town the Sand brothers and Laurie had been to during their violent journey, from Westlock to Nokomis, Wolseley to Russell, and all points in between. Morrison interviewed hundreds of potential witnesses, and believed he had a foolproof strategy for the most important case of his life, a pressure cooker where failure was not an option.

Morrison was being helped by Brandon prosecutor Jim Ross, a long-time Crown in Brandon who paid great attention to detail. Together, Morrison and Ross felt they had left no stone unturned. If they failed to secure convictions, it would not be for lack of trying. Every witness with something to say, no matter how trivial, would testify. Cost would be of no concern, because a police officer was dead, and justice must be done.

Morrison knew the first impression the seven woman, five man jury would get was his opening statement. He wanted the jurors, mostly elderly residents with the ability to suspend their lives for two months and survive on a $30 per diem, to convict Robert and Laurie on the spot, without hearing a single word of evidence. He had spent many long nights leading up to the trial writing and re-writing a summary of the evidence jurors would hear, carefully choosing his words. This was his one chance to tell the world what Laurie and Robert had done to a police officer whose only crime was doing his job. Morrison relished the opportunity.

Morrison developed a common theme in his opening remarks, that of a lurid partnership between Laurie and Robert in which they developed a take-no-prisoners approach towards anyone who got in their way. It was powerful, yet to the point. Morrison began by taking Robert's own words and throwing them directly into the face of the jurors.

"In his diary entry, written the night before Dennis Strongquill is killed, Robert Sand writes 'I've decided on a new approach…. We have so much firepower, that if a cop pulls us over, he will be one sorry motherfucker'," Morrison told the jury. He clearly had their attention. "Well, any policeman in Canada could have been, sorry for the language, that sorry motherfucker."

Robert and Laurie were struck by how raw and aggressive the opening statement was, like something out of a brash American television show or movie. Morrison continued to hammer home the strongest points of his case.

"Dennis Strongquill and Brian Auger approached this traffic stop as routine, the kind they do hundreds of times a year. They were wrong. Tragically wrong."

Morrison pinned much of the blame on Laurie, saying her drug-filled lifestyle caused Robert to throw his own life away, making her the focal point of everything they did. Together, Robert and Laurie formed a vision of an "idyllic life by the sea", he said.

Morrison also told jurors about their sordid background in Alberta, their violent cross-country crime spree, the ambush which left Dennis with nowhere to run, the make-out session in the police station and Robert's confession which proved Dennis's police car became his tomb.

"Constable Strongquill was wildly twisting and turning and thrashing about as he tried to escape a fate he couldn't avoid," said Morrison. "The details of the killing itself are very distasteful. He was seeking the sanctity and safety of the Russell RCMP office. Again, he was tragically wrong."

Morrison finished his opening address by noon, pleased with how it had been delivered, and received. Robert and Laurie were taken back to their private holding cells, to be alone with their thoughts. Morrison's speech replayed in their heads, his words cutting through them like a knife. But their day was only going to get worse.

* * * * * *

After lunch, the police officers who surrounded the Wolseley Motel, the same ones who killed Danny, were called to testify. A dramatic audio tape of the deadly confrontation was played to a hushed courtroom. Robert and Laurie shifted uncomfortably in their seats, hearing the tape for the first time, picturing the scenario in their heads exactly as it unfolded.

Robert bristled as one of the officers on the audio tape described taking Danny out with a single shot to the head, which had caused he and Laurie to give themselves up.

"Two badgers in custody. One cold badger. Two warm badgers," the officer says on the tape. Robert once again pictured his brother, the cold badger, going down for the last time.

When the first day was over, a wave of despair washed over Laurie as she was taken back to her cell in Brandon. She took pen to paper, her thoughts and fears spilling on to the page in a letter she would deliver the next day to Robert at their hiding place in the exercise yard. She had a lot to say, much more than the few minutes each day in court would allow.

Hey Babe. I'm not quite sure what to write. I just want to make sure this gets to you so that we know we can communicate without all those eyes and ears around us. God, do you know how badly I want to reach out to you every time that I see you, how badly I want to hold your hand, to touch you? Oh God, I want to so bad! But I don't want to fuck things up for us even more. I hate to admit it, but I am afraid of the consequences. For our sake and for my family's sake, I'm afraid of how this will end. I cant say I care too much, nor not enough, you know what I mean. This really bites. I'm finally cleaned up and off drugs, I know what I want to do with my life, and I'm afraid that I won't get a second chance at the life I never really had. Cause believe me, the way I used to live was not a life. Ironically, the only thing that I've done that isn't a mistake is loving you, and shit, we even fucked that up. Not the love, that will never change. But the situation that we're in. Maybe in our next life we'll get things right. Cause our love for each other can't be wrong. So, I think that we both have come to accept that neither of us will live in a cage forever. But possibly for the rest of our lives. And then, we will be together again. Don't get me wrong, though, I'm gonna keep on fighting to get out. And if I do, or if I don't, I will always be yours. For us, there is no 'til death do us part', because even death can't keep us apart. I will love you forever. So don't forget that. Just remember our time together. Think about us laying in each other's arms, laughing uncontrollably about nothing and everything. And think about the time the truck got stuck and how you coached me through it by telling me that it's just like making love. Just think about us.

Robert loved hearing from Laurie, a rare bright light in an otherwise dark existence. She knew just what to say, and helped get him through the early days of the trial, which largely focused on Danny's death.

Still in the first week of the trial, an officer named Rod Enns told jurors how he had the grisly task of climbing up to the roof of the Wolseley Motel to check that Danny was dead.

"I was feeling for a pulse, but as soon as I moved him it was clear there was no point in checking. Unfortunately, Mr. Sand was dead," said Enns.

Robert's anger grew, not believing for a second the police felt there was anything unfortunate about Danny's death. Their only regret was that they didn't kill Laurie and him as well.

Danny's death continued to be described in graphic detail to the jurors, which sickened Robert more. Edwin Alport, the doctor who conducted the autopsy, said a single shot fired from about 100 metres away pierced Danny's right cheek, just below the outer side of his right eye. The bullet went through his sinus cavity, skull and out the back of his head, destroying his brain. Death would have been immediate.

* * * * * *

Another letter arrived from Laurie in the early days of the trial.

My love,
Sometimes it still amazes me that we are so perfect for each other. How we are so alike yet so different. I wear my masks as well, I have for as long as I can remember. My family hasn't seen the real me since I was seven years old. These masks I wear, or as I sometimes refer to it as "the game", are what I have to protect myself. It's my armour. I learned how to play the game well when my mother sent me away to an assessment centre for five months when I was 14 to 15 years old. It may seem as thought I am bowing down, but inside I'm not. There are only two ways to life, the easy way and the hard way. I choose the easy way. I'm not bowing down, I'm actually getting what I want

from what is accessible to me. Unfortunately, in this case, there are extreme limits, but I can push those limits without them realizing it. My major problem though is that somewhere along the way I forgot who I was. My mask, my armour, took over, and that's where Tina came from, she was my protection from myself – my past – my childhood. And I needed her, especially on the streets of E-town when I was most vulnerable. There was even a time when Tina completely took over and I couldn't recognize my own reflection in the mirror. Then you found me and saved me from myself. Deep down Tina is still there trying to get out and it is a constant battle. But I know who I am again. When I was Tina, I didn't care if I lived or died, because I lived for the moment, blocking out the rest. It's still hard to face the past. But now I realize that I want my future too. I'm explaining this to you just as much as to myself as well. I've built these walls and I'm slowly taking them down, there is so much I've subconsciously hidden from myself, and now brick by brick I'm learning a lot. But I have to take it one at a time for I fear it will all come crashing down and I will be buried in the rubble. It's like I'm taking these bricks from around myself and rebuilding around Tina. If it all crashes down or if I rebuild too sloppy, she will break free. You've shown me what love is and I don't want to lose that. I want you and I, not our masks. You call me your angel. Well, you are mine too. I want to quote something now that has always had a deep meaning to me. "Every man has his devil, and you can't rest until you find him, and if it's any conciliation, you've put a smile on my face." Well, maybe you're my angel, maybe you're my devil, but you have put a smile on my face, and I can finally rest. If you want to hear my theory, and based on religion, the devil is actually a fallen angel called Lucifer who was banished from the heavens. So you calling me your angel and vice-versa makes the quote about every man and his devil very true in our case. We are each other's destiny, and just as God banished Lucifer from the heavens, the enemy has banished us from each other, but even the Bible says that Lucifer shall rule again (if Christ doesn't get in the way). And we will be together again. Unfortunately, this happens to be our fate, but you are my destiny as I am yours. I will love you in this life and in the next, and in the next. I will love your for all eternity. I don't want the violence anymore, I just want to rest in peace. At the end of this trial we both have to make some choices, and I need you to understand that whatever you choose, I will love you and respect you no less. I understand. I've somehow cheated death too many times to count, and I've always felt there was some unknown reason for my survival. Maybe it was to survive long enough to find the man that I love. And to die knowing that I am loved. Or maybe it is to live being in love, even if we have to stay apart for now, eventually we can be together again. But those are choices we will have to make, either to live with or die with. And know that I will love you for the rest of my life. Whatever choice is made. Yours forever, Angel.

* * * * * *

Robert's friend Elisabeth had been subpoenaed to testify, on behalf of the Crown, about his final days in Alberta before fleeing with Laurie and Danny. The news hit Robert hard, leaving him angry and confused.

Robert picked up the phone, dialling Elisabeth's Edmonton apartment. He still remembered the number, even though they hadn't spoken for months. Robert had wanted it that way. He still loved her deeply, missed her, and wished she could be part of his life. But things were very different now, and it was better if she got on with her own life. Only she wasn't being allowed to do that. Robert resented the Crown for getting her involved in this, vowing they would pay.

The conversation began awkwardly; Elisabeth was surprised to hear from Robert. He had called collect, and she accepted the charges. Robert sounded distant, and distraught. Elisabeth had been following the trial over the Internet, and in Edmonton news reports, and knew things weren't going well for him. But she had no idea how deep his despair had become.

Elisabeth mentioned coming to visit Robert in jail when she was out in Brandon to testify. It would be the first time in 18 months that they would be in the same room. Robert quickly dismissed the suggestion, refusing to put her on a list of approved visitors. Without it, she would be barred entry.

"I really don't care anymore if I live or die," Robert said, his tone frightening Elisabeth. He said it had been a mistake to call her, and that he had to go.

Before hanging up the phone, he had some chilling last words.

"You probably won't hear from me again."

CHAPTER ELEVEN

Robert and Laurie looked forward to the frequent breaks during the trial, usually three or four recesses each day for jurors to have a coffee, smoke a cigarette or answer nature's call. From their prisoner's boxes, which were only about a metre apart, the pair could usually speak to each other in hushed whispers, straining their necks and leaning over as much as the leg shackles would allow. Most meetings were spent giggling about private jokes, each other's appearance, and whether each had received the other's most recent letter.

Robert, feeling particularly lonely and sex-starved one day, wrote a cheeky note to Laurie, asking her to flash him in court. But a sheriff's officer caught them passing the note. Unfortunately for Robert, the only thing Laurie flashed was a smile. Days later, Laurie more than made up for it when a steamy letter arrived in the usual spot at the exercise yard. They may have been on trial for murder, but Robert and Laurie had other things on their minds.

Oh my love. I do dream about you, even when I'm awake. I dream of your hard body pressed against mine while your kisses trail down my neck, down my body as you slowly circle my nipples with your tongue, then one at a time you take them into your mouth, nibbling softly. The smell of your skin makes my heart flutter and I can't

*repress a soft moan of delight as I feel the warmth and wet-
ness between my thighs. Your hands glide down the sides
of my body then back up again to hold me tight in our
lovers embrace, I pull away only long enough to look into
your eyes and whisper "I love you" though its no secret. I
pull you close to kiss you softly at first, them more and
more fiercely, my body aching to feel you fully posses my
body as you do my heart. I feel your fingers tracing the
curves of my breasts, then your hands moving lower trail-
ing them with your kisses until you reach the silky hair of
my womanhood. You gently flick your tongue over my clit
and I cry out with pleasure. I reach down and run my
hands through your long hair as you explore my womanhood with your tongue, then oh so gently probe inside me
with your finger while still tasting me. I want you to take
me so badly, but not quite yet. I pull you up to me again
and as I kiss you deeply I can taste my own sweetness as I
rake my teeth on your bottom lip as I pull away. You roll
onto your back, now its my turn...Now it is my kisses trail-
ing down your neck, down your muscular stomach, then I
moisten my lips and look up into your eyes as I stroke
your manhood with my tongue, slowly up one side, circle
around the tip, then down the other side, and back up
again, only this time I take you into my mouth, teasing at
first, pulling away a few times to flick my tongue over the
tip of your manhood. Then again I take you in my mouth
again, moving in a circular. Up and down, slowly at first,
then faster, more intense, I love the way you taste. My own
body is crying out for my need to feel you deep inside me.
As if you read my thoughts, you gently pull me back into
your arms, you move your body to cover my own and
without hesitating you bury yourself inside me, thrusting,*

again and again, our bodies moving together in perfect ecstasy. I can feel myself getting closer to climax and you feel it too. Together we become one. Afterwards we lay spent in each others arms and as I am drifting off into a blissful sleep, I hear you whisper to me that you love me. After that my dreams are of only you. Love your Angel. P.S. – Tonight I'm sleeping naked for you, but before I sleep I'll be thinking only of you, and when I do sleep tonight I will be dreaming of only you. Hugs and kisses. I love you.

Laurie certainly knew how to put a smile on Robert's face, even if it was from a distance. But her positive outlook, her dreams of being together, only made it harder for Robert to accept his fate. His mood began to darken, evil thoughts running through his mind. He focused on Crown attorneys Bob Morrison and Jim Ross, who seemed to take great joy in sticking it to him. Robert's anger was growing every day, consuming his every thought.

* * * * * *

The case was proceeding smoothly for the Crown, each witness adding another small piece to the bigger puzzle. Although some pieces were clearly larger then others, like the video of Robert and Laurie in a tearful embrace, taken in the police interview room. The uncomfortable images had disgusted some of the jurors, and the Crown was quick to point out the video was shot barely 24 hours after Dennis Strongquill has been killed.

Morrison, staying true to his game plan, made a few editorial statements disguised as questions. Good lawyers knew how to stretch the limits of what they can do in court, and Morrison was one of the best. As the video played, he asked where the concern for Dennis was, knowing none was expressed by Robert and Laurie on tape. True, the video did portray the pair as human beings, young, scared lovers with real feelings and emotions, and that would be a risk. But Morrison and Ross truly believed the sight of them fawning over each in a police interview room while facing murder charges would be hard to ignore.

Robert was doing a slow burn in his prison cell, his hopes of a future with Laurie becoming more unlikely each day, the prospect of rotting in prison for the rest of his life almost inevitable. He was becoming further detached from those around him, choosing to say very little to the sheriff's officers assigned to guard him, shutting out his own lawyers, who would tell him, with a smile, that things were going okay, not to get down, to keep his chin up. But even Laurie's letters, filled with so much hope, couldn't change his mood.

Hey babe. So, have I told you that I love you lately? Yes, I know I have, but I just wanted to tell you again that I love you, because I do, and do you know how crazy you are making me! I think a lot about what we should have been able to have in our life. Marriage, children, a nice little place out in the country somewhere, you know, grow a garden. Actually, when we were arrested I was late and I prayed and prayed that I was pregnant, but no such luck. And depending what the outcome of the trial is, we may still have that chance, if I get out that is. And I have thought about names. I'm not sure what you think about it, but if we have a son, I would like to name him after Dan. And as for choices, my love, I won't be able to make my life or death choices until I'm faced with them. I want to see this trial through. I still have a feeling that I will get out, and if I don't, I will appeal. I've told you that already. And if I do

get out, then I still want to be your wife, have your chil-
dren, and grow a little garden. And that will depend on
your decisions, to. But I've told you again and again, that
I will always be your girl, and If I get out and you chose to
live, then you have to know, that our children will always
know who their father is and how much I love you. It may
be a difficult way to live, but baby, I promise you that I will
always be yours and I will spend my life with you. You will
know our children, and babe, it won't be easy. Life isn't
easy! But we will make it. Our love is that strong! Love, for
all eternity, Angel. XOXO.

* * * * * *

April quickly turned to May, and Robert and Laurie sensed a
shift in the climate, both inside and outside the court. The
buds on the trees, visible through the courthouse windows,
soon gave way to lush greenery. The air felt cooler inside the
court – air conditioning season, a clear indicator it was heating
up outside. In court, the evidence was quickly piling up against
the pair. The Crown finally called its star witness against
Laurie – Rose Ferguson.

This was do or die for Morrison and Ross, whose case
against Laurie rested entirely on the credibility of Ferguson.
The defence would come hard at her, but Morrison felt she
was up for the task. Robert knew these were tough times for
Laurie, and wished he could hold her in his arms, just like he
had when she was fighting the drugs. He figured his fate was
sealed – he hoped Laurie wasn't about to join him.

Nervous, and speaking in a hushed voice, the petite native
woman calmly told the jury how Laurie confessed to playing a
key role in Dennis Strongquill's murder, even joking about the

shooting. It was powerful testimony which left Laurie stunned, Robert livid.

"She told me they had no evidence against her that would keep her in jail. She figured she would walk a year ago," Ferguson testified. "To me, it didn't matter that a person died. She didn't care. She wasn't sorry for what she did to that police officer."

Ferguson recounted the lengthy history of the crime, including the spree of arsons, car thefts and robbery in Alberta and Saskatchewan. Her attention to detail was impressive. Ferguson told jurors Laurie became very talkative once they were lodged together in the Brandon jail cell in early 2002. Laurie described how she and the Sand brothers chased after the police vehicle, ramming it outside the RCMP detachment, while her boyfriend callously pumped four shotgun blasts into Dennis Strongquill's chest.

"She told me she could hear the bullets whizzing past her head and bouncing off the truck. She was yelling at Rob and Danny to 'Kill him, kill him'. That's when Strongquill was shot," said Ferguson.

Reporters covering the high-profile case couldn't write the words fast enough – *Kill Him, Kill Him.* It would be the next day's front page headline in newspapers across the country, which were having a field day with the case, and the incredible access to exhibits such as the video confession and audio of the emergency response team stakeout of the Wolseley Motel. On this day, the story got even better when the Crown tendered as evidence a smiling picture of a pig-tailed Laurie Bell, taken mere hours after her arrest. Laurie had become the poster child for callous indifference.

Ferguson denied defence accusations she was offered incentives to testify, noting that criminal charges she was facing were not affected in any way. Her claims were backed up by several justice officials, who took the witness stand and denied making any deals with Ferguson. Even distant members of her own family, who work in the Dakota Ojibway Police Service, an independent Aboriginal law enforcement agency in Manitoba, denied giving her any information or advice. But the connection to police, however remote, would form a key part of the defence argument.

Laurie could only watch helplessly as Ferguson, a woman she barely knew, told stories which could alter the rest of her life. Her lawyer, Brian Midwinter – who had been quiet up to this point while the more experienced Greg Brodsky did most of the work – had been waiting for the opportunity to tear Ferguson apart. That time had now arrived.

Painting her as a drunk, a liar and a bad mother, Midwinter was relentless. Like a powerful steam engine which takes awhile to get going, Midwinter's intense cross-examination of Ferguson had Laurie feeling better about her plight. Ferguson admitted to a lengthy criminal record, spanning some 17 years, including crimes of deceit. She once left her own young children alone in a house while she went drinking. She was kicked out of university for being a drunk. These were not things that would sit well with a jury. After nearly two full days of grilling Ferguson, Midwinter finally sat down, content that he had more than made his point. Laurie was feeling pretty good as well.

* * * * * *

The day Robert dreaded had finally arrived: Elisabeth would be testifying against him. She walked into court, and still looked so beautiful, dressed in a sharp black suit, her blonde hair cut short. Obviously uncomfortable, Elisabeth told jurors she had just completed a correctional services training program, and was about to become a prison guard. Robert couldn't help but think about the different paths their lives had taken.

His hatred for the Crown attorneys only grew stronger as he watched Elisabeth recall her past with him and Danny, and her communication with the brothers in the days before the killing. *How dare they bring her to court, make her take the witness stand?*

This was all becoming too much, as Sharon Ford was called to testify right after Elisabeth had finished. Now she was involved in this mess. Sharon clearly didn't want to be in court, but Robert was proud of how she held up. He smiled inside as Sharon told jurors that everything was Danny's fault – she was just looking out for him, like she always did. When he was arrested after the shooting, Sharon had been one of the first people he called, just to let her know what had happened. Now on the witness stand, Sharon told jurors that Danny was the leader of the pack, and how she was stunned when he told her that he wouldn't be taken alive.

"I thought he belonged in a hospital for the criminally insane," said Sharon.

As the trial dragged into mid-May, four weeks in, an increasingly despondent Robert asked his lawyers if he could see the pictures the jury had been given, the ones of Danny and Dennis and the crime scene. Robert had been thinking a lot about both men, and felt he needed to see pictures to resolve some issues in his mind. As he flipped through a large evidence book containing nearly 300 different crime scene photos, Robert came across a grisly, close-up picture of Dennis. His limp body was riddled with pellets and fragments, his skin pale and withered. Several pictures followed, from different angles. Robert studied each one, taking in the damage he'd caused to this man he didn't even know. There was no longer a police uniform on Dennis, just bloodied, battered skin. Robert began to write in his diary.

I was looking at this man, on a table. And he had several shotgun wounds, to the side, back, chest, etc. And I started to think, he's just a man, and shouldn't be dead. He had a family and friends, and now he's a body on a table. I realized it's not the man I hated, but the uniform he wore. His flag, colours of war. But seeing him without his uniform I felt bad for the loss of his life.

Robert continued flipping through the book, and didn't go much further before he saw the pictures of Danny. The sight of the head wound which killed him instantly made Robert sick, as he flashed back to the final moments on the roof of the motel.

I flipped to the pics of Dan, and my thoughts changed. Cuz now I felt that the other man is right where he should be. And losses on both sides are always expected, only Dan took my place. And when I looked up the cop car I felt pride, and rememberd the battle. I remembered how these enemy soldiers fled in fear and cowardess. I saw how much damaged I'd causes to there unit and smiled, from the knowledge, that the enemy isn't as strong as they want us to believe. But they should beware that the moment they fly there flag, wear there uniform. That there at war and people die in war, everyone has there enemies.

* * * * * *

Jail officials at the Brandon Correctional Institute first noticed the missing razor blade in mid-May – a cause for major alarm.

In the wrong hands, a razor could be as good as a loaded gun.
And in jail, there were plenty of wrong hands.

Guards had always viewed Robert as a security threat –
shooting a police officer and then trying to escape from jail
made him a maximum risk. As the trial wore on, concerns
were heightened about his potential for violence. All signs
pointed to Robert doing something drastic. Common sense
suggested he likely had nothing left to live for; his brother was
dead, the first-degree murder charge seemed a lock, and he
may never again see the woman he claimed to love. His
previous escape attempt, and suspicious looking fingernails,
were also worrisome. Robert had been growing his nails long,
and appeared to have filed one of them down, creating a sharp,
pointed tip. Prisoner's rights meant Robert could groom
himself as he pleased, even if it sent chills up the spines of
people forced to work with him on a daily basis.

Almost immediately upon discovering a blade was missing,
jail officials began a search of Robert's cell. No razor was
found, but the visit wasn't without some major rewards.
Guards found Laurie's stack of letters, and Robert's latest diary
entries, sitting loose inside the cell. They turned over the
items to the Crown, and Morrison and Ross were thrilled.
Once again, Robert was proving to be his own worst enemy.

* * * * * *

Jurors began hearing about the final days leading up to the
murder, as the Crown paraded witnesses from Alberta,
Saskatchewan and Manitoba to testify about their often violent
encounters with Robert, Danny and Laurie. Defence lawyers
had tried to suppress this evidence before the trial began,
arguing it would prejudice the jury by referring to crimes other

than Dennis's murder. Morrison and Ross argued successfully that the so-called narrative evidence was crucial to proving the trio had everything to lose should they be stopped by police, and that their pattern of violence was escalating to the point of no return.

Testimony reached an emotional peak in late May when a tearful Brian Auger was forced to recount his partner's violent death, and his own tale of survival. Brian was a mess on the stand, speaking in hushed tones and hardly able to look at Morrison, Ross or anyone seated in the packed courtroom.

Brian told jurors about the routine traffic stop, which had been his call to make. It was only supposed to take a few minutes, as he and Dennis made their way to Russell for coffee. His voice cracking, Brian painfully recalled his desperate cries for help from other officers, which went unanswered until it was too late.

"I thought I was going to be killed," he said quietly, staring down at the wooden courtroom floor.

Defence lawyers wisely held off on ambushing the obviously distraught man, deciding there was nothing to gain by trying to make him anything but a tragic victim. Jurors were clearly moved, some reduced to tears. Brian left the courtroom and sat alone in the long narrow hallway, weeping silently.

Jennifer Pashe was the next witness. She also broke down on the stand while recalling how she arrived on scene, only to find Dennis dead. Jennifer finished testifying and left court to find Brian still waiting outside, seated on a bench. He stood up, opening his arms and wrapping her in them. The two officers stood together, faces buried in each other's bright red uniforms, crying over their loss.

* * * * * *

It seemed too easy, slipping the shiny piece of metal past sheriff's officers on a daily basis these past few weeks, clutching it tightly in his hands while sitting in the prisoner's box, watching the Crown call its case, studying their moves, their moods.

Whether he stuffed it in the roof of his mouth, or hid the blade in a shoe, Robert didn't even worry anymore that it would be found. He had beat the security system, if you could call it that, and he was armed. The best part was nobody had a clue. Oh sure, people at the jail knew the razor blade had gone missing, but they hadn't found it, had they? But they would see it soon enough.

It was now early June, and the jury was going to be charged any day now. Robert knew he would be convicted. Thinking otherwise was foolish. Robert was most worried about Laurie, who seemed to be holding up okay, but was clearly terrified about her future. Unlike Robert, long-term jail was foreign to her, and Laurie would not hold up well if she had to spend much more time behind bars. Robert never dreamed she could be convicted, but Morrison and Ross had put in a compelling case, playing to the hearts of the jurors. He hated them for this.

For weeks, Robert had sat silently, watching Morrison and Ross, wanting to hurt them, believing they were smirking and sneering at him. He had been waiting for an opportunity, but knew his options were limited. On either side of him sat sheriff's officers, two large men he sensed were waiting for him to try something. They seemed to want a confrontation. They were going to get it.

* * * * * *

Morrison was in rare form during his final argument on Wednesday, June 11. He summarized how Robert and Laurie made their way from Alberta to Manitoba with no regard for anyone but themselves, in love but out of control. He reviewed the videotaped confession to police, and the time they spent together in the interview room.

"It was a remarkable, and some might say, disgraceful, performance. Constable Strongquill is barely cold and they are snuggling," said Morrison.

He took aim at Laurie, saying the entire ordeal had been one great adventure for her. "In some cases, love and loyalty can be very dangerous," said Morrison. "Robert Sand and Laurie Bell were locked in a dangerous embrace that made the result almost impossible to avoid. They entered a state where the only thing that was important was them. It didn't matter who they hurt."

Morrison described the pair as partners in love, partners in crime. "By all accounts, Robert Sand had been doing quite well…But what in the world could have caused this rapid turn-around in Robert Sand's behaviour? The answer is Laurie Bell. She became the catalyst for everything that happened from there," he said. "However, this was not the stuff of a Harlequin romance novel."

He said the botched bank robbery in Thorhild, followed by the break-and-enter in Nokomis, marked a significant turning point for the fugitives. "They had fled the province, armed themselves, and the death of someone like Constable Strongquill became inevitable. They knew that as soon as they were stopped by police, they faced ruin," said Morrison. "In their worst nightmare, Dennis Strongquill and Brian Auger could not have seen the danger that lay ahead from three suspects with a truckload of weapons and a hatred for the police. They may as well have stopped at the gates of Hell that night."

It was a compelling analogy, one Morrison had been saving to put an exclamation point on his case. He also pointed to forensic evidence which proved Laurie and Robert both handled the guns involved in Dennis's shooting. Morrison told jurors the evidence left no doubt both Robert and Laurie were guilty of a planned and pre-meditated murder of a police officer. To close, he used Robert's own words to make his case, from the cryptic diary entries to the videotaped confession. He urged jurors to trust Rose Ferguson. Yes, she may be a drunk, a liar and a bad mother, but that didn't mean she couldn't tell the truth.

Since neither Robert nor Laurie took the stand to testify – their lawyers knew exposing them to cross-examination in front of a jury was potential suicide – it was easy to put thoughts into their client's heads.

Brodsky did what he could for Robert, but conceded the inevitable to the jurors: his client did indeed kill Dennis Strongquill. He asked jurors to consider the lesser charge of manslaughter, saying the evidence wasn't clear that Robert ever saw Dennis in the police car. He reminded jurors that Robert was open and honest with police in his video state-ment, and had claimed he was just trying to disable the car. It was a stretch, for sure, and Robert knew it. But better to try, and fail, then to not try at all.

Laurie's lawyer took a more aggressive position, claiming the Crown had not made out any case at all against his client. Ferguson was completely unreliable, and her testimony should be dismissed. Midwinter's argument would be given a boost by the judge, who was required by law to give jurors a strong, and lengthy, warning about the questionable nature of informant evidence and how extreme caution must be used at all times. Midwinter capped his closing by arguing for an outright acquittal, saying Laurie was only guilty of being along for the ride.

"She was only there. Being there isn't a crime. What she knew, what she was thinking, was a matter of pure speculation on the Crown's behalf," he said. "What was a girl from Northern Alberta on a road trip to do? There is no way she could conceive in her mind that these men would turn into killers on the side of a blustery highway just days before Christmas."

* * * * * *

Thursday, June 12. Menzies was preparing to deliver his final charge to the jury, putting Robert and Laurie's fate in their hands. Time was running out. Holding the razor blade in the palm of his hand, Robert knew today was the day he must act.

During a mid-morning court recess, while the judge and jurors were out of the room, Robert saw his chance.

Seated to his right, about three metres away, were the men he had grown to hate. Morrison and Ross had their backs turned, and Robert knew he could get to them in a split-second. His first hurdles were the large wooden prisoner's box and the steel shackles on his feet. Seated directly in front of him was Brodsky's assistant, Jason Miller, his back also turned. Robert liked Miller, who had come to visit him in jail on several occasions, to discuss the case and any concerns he had. The two got along well, and Robert felt as if Miller sincerely cared about him. But that didn't matter, not today. Miller was just another obstacle to overcome.

Robert was ready. He leapt out of the box, landing on his feet, directly behind Miller. He reached out, trying to maintain his balance, and caught his lawyer by the throat. They immediately fell to the ground.

Stunned sheriff's officers had somehow missed his jump, but now turned to the commotion beside them. Several rushed over, and put vice-like grips on Robert's head, neck and upper body. Robert could feel the pain, but he was operating on pure adrenaline.

Laurie, seated in the box beside him, shrieked in fear. She jumped on the back of a female sheriff's officer, then fell to her feet. The officer rushed to help in the melee, leaving Laurie alone. She shuffled several steps forward, towards the judge's bench, before she was grabbed. Robert continued to struggle on the ground, losing his razor blade, but now digging his sharpened fingernail into Miller's neck. Sheriff's officers screamed at him to let go.

"Let me go or I'll cut his throat," Robert gasped.

But this was Robert's last attack on authority. He was overpowered, pulled off Miller and dragged roughly out of the court.

Miller, his neck bright red, slowly got to his feet. The other lawyers, including Brodsky, came to Miller's aid, consoling him. Brodsky told his junior to go to the hospital, to get a tetanus shot. A visibly shaken Miller left the courthouse, never to return. Not even for the verdict.

* * * * * *

Robert calmed down. His plan to attack Morrison and Ross had failed, thwarted by his own lawyer. Robert didn't even know what he'd do with them had he reached them, only that he wanted to send a message. He likely wouldn't have cut their throats, but then again, maybe he would have. An angry but composed Brodsky came to visit him during the break, telling Robert he understood his tension but attacking his lawyer in court was no way to deal with it. Deep down, Brodsky was shocked, having never witnessed anything like this.

Robert apologized, agreeing to return to court and be on his best behaviour. He was then handcuffed and shackled so thoroughly that one lawyer said he looked like he had been "Hannibal Lectered".

Justice John Menzies walked briskly back into the courtroom. He was horrified upon hearing of the attack. Before bringing the jury back, he told Robert to think long and hard about what he'd just done.

"I frankly don't care what you do to yourself. But what about Laurie? You say you love her," said Menzies. He told Robert he risked causing a mistrial, and possibly forcing Laurie to sit in jail longer than necessary.

The jurors were brought back in, apparently unaware of the wild commotion. Laurie was now sitting several metres away, as sheriff's officers had separated the prisoner's boxes, moving them apart for the first time since the trial began. Robert looked over, but Laurie didn't return his glances, staring straight ahead, tears welled up in her eyes. As Menzies began his final address, Robert was filled with a sense of despair and loss that he could no longer handle. Weak to the point he could no longer sit, or stand, Robert summoned Brodsky, saying he was too ill to continue. Court was adjourned. The case would end the next day – Friday, the 13th.

* * * * * *

The news rocketed through Brandon. The jury had a verdict. It was 6 p.m, only a few hours since they had begun deliberating. Everyone who followed the case figured Robert's verdict would only take minutes, maybe seconds – it seemed that straight forward. But Laurie was a different story, and there was a belief the case might stretch into the weekend. But whether it was the predicted daytime highs of 30°C, or the clarity of the case, jurors apparently didn't need much time to reach a consensus.

Robert heard the news, but was barely able to process it. Still feeling the effects of the courtroom catastrophe, he had voluntarily agreed to take a dose of sedatives, leaving him disoriented and weak. Laurie was in better spirits, but was battling a myriad of emotions from the previous day. For the first time, she had been genuinely frightened by Robert's actions, to the point she had begun questioning her relationship with him. The thoughts had never really entered her mind after Dennis was killed. But they were now. And with her own freedom at stake, it was almost too much to bear.

Laurie did get a boost with the arrival of an unexpected visitor. Donna Bell had flown in from Athabasca to be with Laurie in the final days, and Laurie was thrilled to see her mother. An optimistic and forgiving Donna told Laurie she had come to take her back to Athabasca. Eighteen months ago she couldn't wait to flee her family – now there was nothing she wanted more then to be able to go back home.

The courtroom gallery quickly filled, with media, other lawyers, police officers and members of the public who had followed the case from start to finish. Dennis Strongquill's family had spent the day together, on the front lawn of a Brandon home, sipping lemonade, soaking up the sun and looking at old pictures of Bosom. They had been waiting for the phone to ring with news of a verdict, trying to pass the time with a trip down memory lane. Now the call had come.

Security was beefed up, as two armed, undercover officers were posted in the courtroom, just in case Robert tried anything. Sheriff's officers had their guard up, planning for the worst but hoping for the best.

A hush fell over the court, more than 100 people barely making a sound. It had been nearly an hour since it was learned a verdict was in, and the tension was thick. Finally, just before 7 p.m., Menzies entered the courtroom. He called in the jurors, who slowly walked from a back room and found their seats, looking right away at Robert and Laurie. Menzies asked the foreman to rise. An older man in the front row, juror number two, got up.

"Have you reached a verdict?" Menzies asked.

"We have, your honour," the man replied.

Robert's was first up, his charge to be read aloud by the clerk.

"To the charge of first-degree murder, how do you find?" the woman asked sternly.

The foreman wasted no time.

"Guilty!" he bellowed.

Dennis's family, including sisters, cousins, nieces and nephews, erupted with joy. Cries of "thank you" and loud clapping filled the courtroom.

Robert slumped over, the drugs slowing his reaction but not numbing it. He buried his head in his hands. It was all over, at least for him. But Laurie still had hope.

Laurie clutched her hands together tightly, exchanging nervous glances with her lawyer.

The first-degree charge was read.

"Not guilty," the foreman said.

An audible gasp was heard from Dennis's family in the back of the courtroom.

The clerk read out the second option – second-degree murder.

"Not guilty," the foreman said again.

Morrison and Ross shifted in their seats, looking uncomfortable.

The third option – manslaughter. Laurie held her breath. There was a pause, which seemed to last forever.

"Guilty," the man said.

A faint smile washed over Laurie's face, while another cheer came from the gallery. In the back, Donna Bell quietly walked out of court, her tinted sunglasses hiding whatever emotion she was feeling.

* * * * * *

Before Robert would be formally sentenced, Morrison and Ross submitted a victim impact statement, which had been penned by Dennis Strongquill's sister, Ruby Brass, on behalf of his entire family. Brass had poured her heart into the document, just as Dennis put his entire soul into everything he did.

Today I write this impact statement with a heavy heart. The past one and a half years has been one of hatred for the accused. I have tried to understand how someone can take a person's life with no remorse or compassion. My initial reaction was to hurt the accused so they could feel the pain I have been feeling.

My family and I have tried to lead a normal life since the death of my brother. But have no succeeded too well, myself personally I have been placed on anti-depressant medication to control my emotions and feelings. I cannot sleep at night – only to have nightmares about him getting shot (over and over). I have not been able to focus on my own goals or my family until I can see this through (find a job, focus on my children and their needs).

Dennis and I both lived our lives to help others who could not help themselves. We have tried to instil this passion in our children, but it makes us feel less trusting for those who can't help themselves.

My children and family are grieving and have turned to me but I can not be there for them completely because I am suffering myself. There have been times during the last year and a half where we have created tension and chaos and hurt feelings, negativism towards each other – while there was none before all this happened.

I will no longer be able to see my brother's smiling face, hear his laughter, feel his pain, hear him cry, hear him sing, hear his stories of his love for his children and feel the love that was there because he is gone. (dead)

Dennis was a role model for the community and for his children. He was very proud to have worn the uniform of an RCMP officer. We are very proud of him. We were not ready for Dennis to leave us, it was too premature and unfair. He was proud to be a new father but now he will not be able to fulfill that role.

It has been a very long and hard journey for us all. Maybe now we can find some peace and let Dennis complete his journey home.

Robert had nothing to say when Menzies called on him, offering his one and only chance to clear his conscience. There was no discretion in the sentencing – first-degree murder meant mandatory life in prison with no chance of parole for 25 years – so making a speech in court couldn't help Robert anyway. Still, members of Dennis's family wished he would at least say something, try in some small way to explain himself. But Robert, who could barely stay on his feet because of the medication, remained seated, his mouth shut.

Menzies called the case "a terrible waste of life" and tore into Robert for his attack on Miller, calling it incomprehensible and mind-boggling. "You are not a stupid man. You are an intelligent man. The only conclusion I can come to is that you hate society. You can't tolerate authority. You hate the police," Menzies said, his voice dripping with anger.

"In your diary, you said this was war. But this wasn't war. It isn't war when only one side knows about it."

He then lowered the boom on Robert, telling him life in prison was exactly what he deserved.

Robert showed no emotion, and his only response was to leave the courtroom with the help of sheriff's officers. Laurie remained seated in the prisoner's box, staring directly ahead as Robert shuffled slowly through the courtroom, his back to her. Their eyes never met. They likely never would again.

CHAPTER TWELVE

Laurie was alone in court for the first time, now at the mercy of the judge. It had been two weeks since a jury convicted her of manslaughter, yet her fate remained a mystery. Her lawyer, Brian Midwinter, was going to try and get her out of jail as quickly as possible, but was facing an uphill battle. Although manslaughter sentences in Manitoba have gone as low as 18 months, the killing of Dennis Strongquill was hardly the typical drunken fight which usually qualifies for such leniency.

Crown attorney Bob Morrison had tried his best to put Laurie away for life, but the first-degree murder prosecution had failed. Clearly, the testimony of Rose Ferguson was dismissed by the jurors, a result not surprising given the strong warning by the judge and gruelling cross-examination that exposed their star witness against Laurie as a lying drunk. Morrison, however, didn't feel like he'd lost anything. Robert Sand had been found guilty as charged, and would be locked away from society for the next 25 years, at least. He might never get out. Danny Sand was dead, the ultimate punishment for his brutal acts. And Laurie was still going to pay a price. Morrison planned to ask for 10 more years.

Wearing black jeans and a white long-sleeve shirt, Laurie had let her hair down for the first time since the trial began.

Gone were her signature pigtails, which had portrayed a sense of sweetness, innocence and youth and contradicted the brutal act she had participated in. But the jury was now out of the picture, save for a few of the 12 who had returned to court on this final day of June to sit in the public gallery and watch Queen's Bench Justice John Menzies pass sentence.

Robert was also gone, both from the courtroom and her life. Laurie, of course, hadn't been able to speak with him since the verdict came down two weeks earlier – a personal decision made even easier by the fact logistics wouldn't allow it. She had come to accept this, ready to move on to a new chapter in her young life. But the story still wasn't finished.

In court to be sentenced, there was now only one prisoner's box, and a noticeably reduced security presence. Robert was no longer a threat, and he would soon be heading east to a super-maximum prison in Quebec to be placed with some of Canada's worst killers and most dangerous inmates. Laurie was headed west, but whether it was on her own free will or in custody remained to be seen.

"Some people thought this was the trial of Pippi Longstocking," Morrison said at the beginning of his sub-mission, an obvious jab at Laurie's appearance which had many in the courtroom chuckling quietly. "But she is no Pippi Longstocking."

Morrison called Laurie a "parent's worst nightmare" and told Menzies she had been found guilty of one of the worst manslaughters imaginable. Only the sex killing of a child tops the slaying of a police officer, he said. "Our whole society mourns a case like this. Our whole society is outraged. And they look to this court to make a statement," said Morrison.

Morrison keyed on Laurie's letters to Robert, saying she was more concerned with putting a smile on her boyfriend's face then with the tragic death of an honourable man.

"Some of these letters, as she shares her sexual fantasies, would be more appropriate for an adult magazine."

Morrison was tempted to ask for life in prison for Laurie – the maximum sentence allowed by law which would require her to serve at least seven years before being eligible for parole – but said her young age and lack of a serious criminal record restricts him from doing so. But he encouraged Menzies to look beyond any claims from Laurie and her lawyer that she was simply along for the ride. "Laurie Bell obviously knew the dream she had together with Robert Sand would fail upon their first encounter with police."

Midwinter was next, and went hard at his claim that Laurie never knew the kind of violence Robert was capable of. He played off Robert's conviction and Danny's death, saying proper punishment had already been meted out. "The primary actor in this sorry set of events has already been found guilty and sentenced."

Midwinter argued that since the jury had rejected first and second-degree murder in Laurie's case, the judge could only sentence her on the grounds she never knew somebody would die.

Menzies only needed the lunch hour to decide. He gave Laurie credit for the 18 months she had already served in custody, which Canadian courts count as double-time. Then he piled on seven more years. Morrison had got his 10 years.

"Two very honourable men were brutally attacked that night. They were hunted down. It is an abhorrent crime," Menzies said in passing down the sentence. "This was an attack on the very system that allows you to express hate for police officers. They protect that right for you."

It was a crushing blow, tempered only by the fact she had been facing life in prison only two weeks earlier. Still, she was only 21. This sentence represented one-third of her life. Laurie knew she could get out earlier, on parole, if she was well-behaved and stayed out of trouble, but it seemed like a lifetime away.

In the days that followed, Laurie began to see a faint glimmer of hope. The Crown had no intention of appealing the manslaughter verdict or the seven-year sentence, leaving Laurie with nothing to lose if she launched an appeal of her own. Midwinter filed the paperwork in early July, seeking a hearing before the Manitoba Court of Appeal. He planned to argue the manslaughter verdict was unfit, that Laurie should have walked free. If the province's highest court wouldn't set her free on the spot, Midwinter at least wanted a new trial for Laurie. Because the Crown hadn't appealed, it would only be for manslaughter the second time around, and not first-degree murder.

If that argument failed, Midwinter would fight to reduce the sentence, claiming Menzies had been unduly harsh. Laurie was optimistic, and clung to the belief there were brighter days ahead. But she knew the process was a slow one, and a hearing likely wouldn't be held until 2004. But things could have been worse. She could have been in Robert's shoes.

* * * * * *

The call Elisabeth Colbourne never expected came in early July 2003. Robert was on the line.

It had been nearly two months since Elisabeth had walked nervously in to the Brandon courthouse, looking Robert in the eyes, her heart breaking. His sadness and anger were obvious, and they were the feelings Elisabeth was also struggling to cope with. Robert had made it crystal clear, during their last phone conversation, just before she testified for the Crown, that he didn't want her in his life anymore. It would be easier if they just went their separate ways. But Elisabeth couldn't help but follow the trial, from a distance, through to its violent and painful end.

The conversation started easily enough, with very little said about the trial or its outcome. Robert sounded distant, but shared a laugh with Elisabeth when she mentioned she'd finally got her driver's licence. Robert recalled a traffic ticket he once received.

"I'm surprised I haven't gotten a photo radar ticket yet," she joked.

Robert's tone quickly turned serious, mentioning Danny. He blamed himself for his brother's death, and for Laurie's plight. Robert said he never should have brought them with him.

Towards the end of the talk, Elisabeth asked Robert if he planned to call again. He was still in Stony Mountain penitentiary, just outside of Winnipeg, and would soon be moved to Quebec.

"Probably not," said Robert.

Elisabeth began to cry. "Maybe if things had turned out different…"

"You just don't understand. My mom doesn't understand," said Robert.

There was a pause.

"I love you," said Elisabeth.

Robert didn't hesitate with his answer. "I love you." He hung up the phone.

* * * * * *

Dennis Sand still notices the staring, the whispering, and the second glances from people, part of the daily routine when you're the parent of two cold-blooded killers. Being an employee of the County of Westlock, Dennis can't hide from the public the way he often wishes he could. He has come to accept it, viewing it as punishment for the ways he must have failed his boys. How else to explain what has happened? Dennis doesn't look for blame any further then his own reflection in the mirror, but often wonders about the early years Robert and Danny spent in youth jail, becoming more bitter, not better, as a result.

Elaine Sand spends her days doting on her flower garden, keeping the house trailer tidy or tending to the vegetables in the greenhouse. The days are often long, and lonely, with Dennis away at work and Elaine alone with her thoughts. Their social calendar is quite bare, although that's just the way they like it.

Robert's calls from prison are infrequent at best, something they hope will change one day. Until then, Robert and Danny mainly exist in their memories – two lost souls, two lost sons.

The Sand family did have reason to celebrate, in May 2003, while Robert was still on trial. Dusty, the youngest of the three Sand boys who has taken a remarkably different path than his brothers, married his long-time girlfriend. It was a small, modest wedding. With one brother dead and another in prison, Dusty turned to his bride's family to fill his side of the wedding party. Just like Christmas 2001, Robert and Danny had managed to cast a pall over what otherwise would have been a joyous occassion.

* * * * * *

The Royal Canadian Mounted Police will never forget Dennis Strongquill, or the ultimate sacrifice he made in the course of his duties. A trust fund was established for his children, at the Royal Bank, with hopes of helping them have the future Dennis so desperately would have wanted to provide. Dennis's name was also added to the RCMP Wall of Honour, dedicated to officers who have been killed on the job.

In September 2003, an emotional Brian Auger joined Mandy Delorande and little Korrie at a ceremony in Russell to dedicate a cairn to Dennis. More than 450 people packed the Russell Community Centre, many fighting back tears as the monument carrying Dennis's face was unveiled. Police boots thundered on the floor as the formal ceremony began with a traditional march.

"This is an opportunity for us to show we care very much for what police officers do for us," said Russell Mayor Merril Kiliwnik.

Brian was asked by reporters to describe his thoughts while standing over the cairn, which includes an inscription and the RCMP insignia.

"It is hard to describe. I probably couldn't tell you," he said softly.

Mandy proudly held her daughter, looking up towards the sky, confident Dennis was looking down on them.

The RCMP also wanted to ensure better measures were put in place to prevent another tragedy of this kind. Just weeks after Dennis was killed, the RCMP made it mandatory for all officers to wear their protective bullet-proof vests. Dennis hadn't been wearing his the night he was killed, and took four shots to his chest and back. The jury will forever be out on whether it would have made a difference between life and death, but one thing is clear. Had Dennis been wearing the vest, he at least would have stood a fighting chance.

The RCMP also launched an investigation into Dennis's malfunctioning gun, and the results were shocking. Dennis, a left-handed shot, was using a gun designed for right-handers. The nine-millimetre Glock was mounted on his left hip, exposing a release mechanism for his magazine which would be protected when mounted on the right hip. Somehow, in the chaos and confusion of that snowy winter night, the button was jostled and the ammunition fell to the ground, never to be recovered by a desperate Dennis who was left to stare down Robert Sand with nothing but fear. It was a tragic mistake the RCMP vowed would never happen again. It is now mandatory for left-handed officers to bring their pistols in for modification to protect the release lever from accidental release. On a related matter, it is also mandatory for police-issue shotguns to be in cruisers at all times.

Finally, there was a probe into how Laurie Bell had managed to walk away, her freedom still intact, after her encounter with an RCMP officer in Athabasca, when a warrant should have been issued for her arrest. In fact, the warrant had been issued on December 10, 2001 – one day earlier – but it didn't show up on the police system for days. Several flaws in the system were exposed. Once a warrant is issued by a judge, it goes to a document processing area in the courts, where it can take several days because of understaffing and overwork for a clerk to type it up, then have it reviewed and signed. Once completed, it is then sent to police and likely added to a pile on another data clerk's desk. Eventually, it will be entered into a national police database – but not before giving a criminal like Laurie plenty of time to get away.

* * * * * *

Reminders of Dennis Strongquill are everywhere in Barrows. Inside Mandy Delorande's home, a large oil painting of Dennis hangs above the television in her living room. He is wearing his red RCMP uniform. In the top corner of the painting is little Korrie, looking down at her father. Mandy believes Dennis now looks down at Korrie, who at two is the spitting image of Dennis, with her dark, thick hair and chubby brown cheeks. She is still too young for Mandy to explain what happened to Dennis, but Korrie does go over to the picture and say "Daddy" on occasion. It is often too much for Mandy to bear.

Life does go on, however, and for Mandy that life now includes a new man. His name is Tony, a long-time friend who was there for her after Dennis died. There is talk of marriage, hopefully in May 2004. Mandy and Tony also plan to leave Manitoba behind, following their wedding. Mandy wants to go back to school, upgrade her education and training, while Tony intends to find work on the oil rigs. They plan to move to Whitecourt, which is north of Edmonton. Their new home will not be far from the communities of Westlock and Athabasca, where the Sand brothers and Laurie Bell grew up.

* * * * * *

Robert is in handcuffs and leg shackles, stuck inside a tiny room, when a visitor walks in to the cubicle directly facing him. His greasy hair is pulled tight into a pony tail, his face unshaven and angry. Separated by a large pane of glass, Robert agreed to speak with a newspaper reporter just a few weeks after being convicted of the most serious charge in the Criminal Code. He is in his final days at Stony Mountain penitentiary, and knows darker days are ahead once he gets to

Quebec, where the prisons are notorious hellholes. Robert has plenty to say, and nothing left to lose. He is no longer muzzled by his lawyers, or the threat of hurting Laurie or their trial.

Robert manages a bleak smile as he recalls fooling the sheriff's officers, day after day, by bringing the razor blade to court.

"Security was a joke," he says, disdainfully. He never wanted to hurt his lawyer, Jason Miller, and is sorry he got in the way. He also regrets not reaching his intended targets – Crown attorneys Bob Morrison and Jim Ross.

"I wanted to hurt them. They pissed me off, dragged Laurie through the mud, and turned the trial into a big parade."

He is still seething about the manslaughter verdict for Laurie, and the seven years in prison she received.

"She never should have even been on trial. She didn't do anything. A trial is supposed to be about truth and justice. Well, I didn't see any of that."

The reporter asks Robert about comparisons to other notorious Canadian killers, such as Paul Bernardo. Robert's face instantly turns to disgust.

"Paul Bernardo is a piece of shit."

He also rejects any similarities to the fictional characters of Mickey and Mallory in the dark Hollywood movie, *Natural Born Killers*. Robert has seen the movie, enjoyed it actually.

"Mickey and Mallory were killing anybody and everybody. They were doing it for notoriety. I never killed no Ma and Pa in some grocery store. If this was *Natural Born Killers,* everybody in that bank in Alberta would have been dead."

Robert begins speaking of his regrets. Danny would still be alive, and Laurie would have her freedom, if it wasn't for him. Deep down, Robert knew a confrontation with police was inevitable. All those encounters over the years had placed a target on the police as far as Robert was concerned. He planned to fight them all along. But bringing Danny and Laurie with him was a tragic mistake.

"I should have gone by myself, I could have hid out, lived in the bushes, survived on my own. I had something to take care of, and I regret taking them along."

Robert also blames himself for what he has done to his parents, Dusty, and Elisabeth. But he has no plans to let them into his life in any big way.

"I have let them down. But who I am now is not the person they remember."

Robert has kept himself occupied by reading, writing and maintaining a daily regimen of 2,000 push-ups. It keeps him strong, physically and mentally. But he doesn't plan on sticking around for much longer, definitely not for the 25 years he must serve before being eligible for parole.

"If I had a purpose I could make 25 years. I could adapt. But what am I going to do when I get out."

He says he doesn't believe in suicide. "But there are lots of ways to die in prison."

Manitoba's justice minister, Gord Mackintosh, doesn't think 25 years is sufficient for the Robert Sands of the world. He is not alone, as many who followed the case believed nothing short of capital punishment is a just sentence. In the weeks that followed Robert's conviction, Mackintosh vowed to lobby Ottawa to strip away parole eligibility for convicted cop killers, making it impossible for them to ever get out of prison. The issue, sure to gain a tidal wave of public support, remains very much alive.

For Robert, hope no longer exists, plans of marriage and a garden by the sea vanquished. Laurie is now a part of his past, his prison sentence the final nail in a relationship which was deeply passionate, but not deeply rooted. Robert is angry some people, including his parents, believe Laurie pushed him over the edge.

"None of this is Laurie's fault, I don't blame her at all. Something like this was going to happen sooner or later, and what happened with her and I just pushed the date forward," Robert tells the reporter.

The interview nearly complete, Robert admits life would be better if he hadn't killed Dennis. He has read the papers, heard the outcry in court, knows the hurt he's caused.

"Everyone in this province has made him out to be a hero. Sure, there are some good cops, but the police officers that fell in my hands that night are the ones I hated, as far as I knew," says Robert.

"But I had nothing against him as a man. If I were to run into him in a bar and he wasn't wearing his uniform, we probably would have shared a beer together."

* * * * * *

Just behind home plate, facing the highway that runs through Barrows, sits a large slab of black granite. Dennis Strongquill grew up on this badly overgrown baseball diamond, and had planned to spend his final days here playing catch with his children. There is really no reason for anyone to stop in this town during their travels, and most people simply pass it by without a second glance. The plaque reads:

STRONGQUILL – This cairn and ball park are dedicated to honour the memory of Const. Dennis Strongquill, who died in the line of duty on Dec. 21/01. Const. Strongquill started as the Barrows and area community constable and served in this area from 1979-1981. Const. Strongquill then went on to serve the RCMP from 1981 to 2001. Const. Dennis Strongquill was well known to the area for his sporting abilities, which included baseball and hockey.

Just a few minutes away is the Whispering Pines Cemetery, where Dennis's gravesite is surrounded by bright-coloured flowers and pine trees, symbolic of the Christmas he never survived to see.

Now mid-summer, a warm breeze blows through the towering pine above the grave, whistling the various wind chimes which hang from the branches. Nearby are the other tombstones of Barrows' dearly departed, a permanent reminder of a community's painful past. But at the top of a grassy hill lies Dennis Strongquill, looking over the community he fought so hard to protect, a fallen hero whose life will always be remembered, but whose fate will never be understood.

A cairn, dedicated to the memory of Dennis Strongquill, is displayed during a September 2003 ceremony in Russell, where he was killed in December 2001. The monument will remain in the western Manitoba town to honour his memory. *(Photo courtesy RCMP)*